© Copyright 2006 Katherine Doe

All rights reserved. No part of this publication may be reproduced, stored in a retrieval system, or transmitted, in any form or by any means, electronic, mechanical, photocopying, recording, or otherwise, without the written prior permission of the author.

Note for Librarians: A cataloguing record for this book is available from Library and Archives Canada at www.collectionscanada.ca/amicus/index-e.html
ISBN 1-4251-0289-1

green power

TRAFFORD
PUBLISHING
Offices in Canada, USA, Ireland and UK

Book sales for North America and international:
Trafford Publishing, 6E–2333 Government St.,
Victoria, BC V8T 4P4 CANADA
phone 250 383 6864 (toll-free 1 888 232 4444)
fax 250 383 6804; email to orders@trafford.com

Book sales in Europe:
Trafford Publishing (UK) Limited, 9 Park End Street, 2nd Floor
Oxford, UK OX1 1HH UNITED KINGDOM
phone +44 (0)1865 722 113 (local rate 0845 230 9601)
facsimile +44 (0)1865 722 868; info.uk@trafford.com

Order online at:
trafford.com/06-2046

10 9 8 7 6 5 4 3 2

This book is dedicated firstly to my parents,
Mary Cecelia Ward and
Ambrose William Taylor
and to my siblings Harvey, Jack, Olga, Bill, Vern,
Jim, Tom and Margaret who contributed in so
many ways to my fun-filled childhood.
It is because of them that I have these memories
to share.

And to my husband Richard L. Doe, the most
courageous man I have ever known.

Lastly, but most importantly, to my children,
Lisa, Richard and Michael and my grandchildren
Brittany, Joshua, Matthew, Makayla,
Adam and Alex.

They are the reason I put these memories down
on paper in the first place.

Introduction

In 2004, when my husband became seriously ill and was bedridden for many months, I knew I needed something to occupy the long hours which, by the seriousness of his illness, forced me to be almost as housebound as he. I had always been a person who at the drop of a hat, drove to the shopping mall, visited friends, taught a few classes at the local college, or went to be with family members without even thinking about it. And suddenly my days and nights were spent mainly inside the walls of the six room home we had recently purchased. This was a move made necessary because of the need for constant upkeep of the twelve-room home we had owned for over forty years, and which, because of its very size, proved too much for my husband to care for any longer.

To help fill the hours that were becoming increasingly lonelier and lonelier, I first tried writing short stories. But after a few chapters, I would lose interest in the topic and attempt a different story line. Finally, I gave up completely and spent most of my time reading every novel I could get my hands on or emailing friends until they were most likely ready to put a block on my email address.

It dawned on me one day that I should write about my *own* life...where I came from, my early years and how I met the man that I was now watching slowly slip away. I realized that this would possibly be of interest to no one but our children and their children, and perhaps their children after them, and they might find it a lot of fun to read. After all, I reasoned, who would not want to know more about their parents and their grandparents? What was their childhood like? What were they thinking and planning when they were growing up, reaching adolescence and finally adulthood? I knew writing it would be interesting to me and I certainly knew the character in the storyline very well. So with all this in mind, I sat down at my computer and began to put some sort of order to my growing years.

Probably the biggest advantage of transferring all these memories to paper is that I finally had something constructive to do to occupy the many long days and nights while working at my computer in a room located next to my husband's bedroom. I could hear the sounds of his snoring as he slept for longer and longer periods of time each day as he became progressively weaker. And when I heard the sound of his electrically operated hospital bed going up, that would be my cue to stop typing and see what he needed.

In addition, the bell that was always on his nightstand could beckon me in a matter of moments. However, as time went on he slept more and more hours and asked for things less and less. Thus, this story was created mostly to the sounds of his silence.

In writing this memoir, I conjured up memories I thought I had forgotten. Some very good and a few not so good but they were memories that belong to me and I wanted to share them with my children. There is a chance that if some of my siblings read this memoir, they may not remember the events that I relate to. This is normal. We all look at our past in different ways. What would seem of no significance to one family member may be remembered for a lifetime by another.

I have heard my own brothers and sisters relate stories about past events that took place when I was old enough that I should remember, but often I did not. But these particular memories belong to me...I lived them, I was affected by them and they were important enough to me to chronicle. I hope my offspring enjoy learning more about their parents, grandparents and aunts and uncles.

Katherine L. Taylor Doe

Table of Contents

Chapter 1	Humble Beginnings
Chapter 2	They Met, They Married, They Moved
Chapter 3	Siblings
Chapter 4	Lights, Camera, Action!
Chapter 5	Older Brothers and Sisters Are Neat
Chapter 6	John Frederick Taylor
Chapter 7	Wash Day Blues
Chapter 8	Jack, We Hardly Knew Ye"
Chapter 9	Mom's Last Residence – Warm At Last
Chapter 10	Stuart Street Meltdown
Chapter 11	Things I'd Rather Forget
Chapter 12	I Get To Be an 'Only Child'
Chapter 13	Losing a Parent
Chapter 14	Love is a Many Splendored Things
Chapter 15	Richard Lawrence Doe
Chapter 16	I Meet the Man I Will Marry
Chapter 17	Introducing Mr. and Mrs. Richard Doe
Chapter 18	Lisa Marie Doe
Chapter 19	Susan Kathleen Doe
Chapter 20	Richard James Doe
Chapter 21	Michael Andrew Doe
Chapter 22	Lights, Camera, Action All over Again
Chapter 23	Eric Joseph Doe
Chapter 24	Parenting, Partying, Having Fun
Chapter 25	Thomas L. Taylor
Chapter 26	Mary Cecilia Ward Taylor
Chapter 27	Harvey E. Taylor
Chapter 28	The Long Wait
Chapter 29	A Letter to My Children

Chapter 1

Humble Beginnings
Faith and Begora or Oy Vey?

If asked what ones very first childhood memory is, a person may relate an incident that took place when he or she was only three or four years old. It could be happy *or* traumatic because both of these strong emotions have the ability to stamp its very identity on the brain, enabling it to be recalled many years later. I myself have tried to conjure up memories before the age of four or five, but cannot seem to remember anything significant. However, I do have a very clear recollection of being eight years old and living in a house on Stuart Street in Watertown, New York, a sleepy city sixty miles north of Syracuse and very close to the frigid Canadian border. Basically, it was because I almost died one day while living within its walls. This event definitely had all the markers necessary for easy recall many years later. Thinking about that today, I can only imagine the fear that my mother experienced when the youngest of her ten children almost met her Maker. But more about that later.

My mother, Mary Cecelia Taylor, was born in 1900 to a 23-year-old woman at St. Mary's Maternity Ward, a hospital on Dean Street in Brooklyn. This hospital was founded in 1858 and run by the Sisters of Charity. Mom's mother was a nurse at that hospital and was not married at the time of Mom's birth. Records show that my grandmother resided in a room at the hospital so she may have still been a nursing student. It's not too difficult to imagine the stigma attached to being found expecting a child in that day and age with no wedding band placed firmly on your left hand.

My grandmother's name was Mary Leavy. Her father Patrick Leavy was born in Ireland in August 1839 and moved to New York City about 1858. Patrick and his wife had three children, Mary (Mom's mother) born in March of 1877, Dellia, born in February 1885, and Joseph born in October 1886. The Leavy family lived at 230 4th Avenue in Brooklyn according to the 1900 Census.

My grandmother Mary Leavy met and dated a man by the name of William Smith. His date of birth was May 1875, making him two years older than Mary. William Smith lived in New York City with his parents. Irish people were and still are notorious for being staunch Catholics and his religion was listed as such. Despite Mary Leavy's religion being recorded as Catholic on her hospital records, it's possible she was related to the Jewish Leavy's that populated many of the Brooklyn neighborhoods in the early part of the century. This little bit of information about whether my brothers and sisters and I are part Jewish titillates us even to this day. Perhaps this is as good a place as any to share a very strange but true event that happened to me regarding my grandmother's possible religious persuasion.

About ten years ago I was teaching a computer class at our local community college. The class was geared towards instructing senior citizens on the mystery of operating a personal computer. In this class was a Watertown physician who was noted for his patience; something he needed a lot of during this four-day class. I say this because seated next to him was a woman of about 80 who was as confusing to converse with as she was brilliant. You could tell that this woman (whom I'll call "Agnes"), came from wealth; was very well spoken, had excellent manners and was very interested in learning about this new marvel, the computer.

But as smart as she was, she also had the strange habit of "flipping out" every so often. For example, Agnes would be speaking to the doctor in a very animated way, truly enjoying his company, then suddenly she would say something so off the wall that it would take him by surprise. I noticed this myself as my teaching podium was located very near to both of them. He would look at me and smile and I would acknowledge with a nod that poor Agnes was becoming a little rattled. But no sooner then we realized it; she was back to her old self and making sense again. In any event, what startled me the most was what Agnes told me during one of our coffee breaks.

She was having a nice chat with some people around her, and then she came up to me and talked for a while about how much she enjoyed the class and the people she was meeting. I asked her where she was from and she told me that she had just arrived in Watertown and was visiting her daughter and son-in-law for a couple of weeks and would be going back home to Florida shortly. Agnes informed me that her family thought it would be good for her to learn how to use the computer so they could begin emailing one another. As the break was almost over, she began to start back to her seat but then suddenly turned towards me as if she had one more thought to share with me.

It was then that Agnes said to me, "You know, your mother was a Jewish girl, most likely by the name of Leavy. They're Jewish people you know...the Leavy's of New York." And at that, she sat down.

To say I was dumbfounded is an exaggeration. I don't remember much of anything else about the remainder of the class. I spent the rest of the time wondering why in the world she said something like that to me when I had been informed by my nephew David Taylor[1] just a few months earlier, that Mom's mother's last name was Leavy. David had shown me Mom's birth certificate which proved it. In thinking about this strange incident today, I guess I would chalk it up to one of life's very strange mysteries.

Mom's parents obviously chose not to marry when they found out they were expecting a child. Perhaps William Smith did not even know of the pregnancy. Or if he did, perhaps both of them felt they could not, or did not want to make the union official.

David also discovered that when Mom was born in February of 1900, her birth certificate shows that her father William Smith was living at 168 Sackett Street (a boarding room house) which is near Dean Avenue and located right around the corner from the hospital in which Mom was born. However, four months later, in June of 1900, the Census does not show him still living there but does show a Mary and William Smith living at 61st Street in southern Brooklyn. These people had the same months and years of births as Mom's parents. David and I both strongly believe that after giving birth to my mother and placing her up for adoption, my grandmother ended up marrying William anyway[2].

I am sure my mother wondered for years if her parents tried to locate her and how many siblings she might have. Family was always very important to Mom so it's easy to assume she would have loved to be a member of a big, Irish Catholic/Jewish family of which both of her parents were most likely a part.

Shortly after my mother's birth, she was sent to the Brooklyn Catholic Orphanage and stayed there until 1906 when she was taken to the home of

---

[1] My brother Bill Taylor's 2nd oldest son and family genealogy expert, to whom I owe much thanks for his assistance in my writing this book.
[2] David plans to check out the Feb. to June 1900 marriage license of nearby churches.

William McEvoy of Sackets Harbor, New York. She remained in his care until around 1915 when she was about 15 years old. William McEvoy died three years later in 1918 at the young age of 49.

Mom then ended up being cared for by a man named Peter J. Ward. This gentle man, who was affectionately known as Grandpa Ward to us, was born in Edinburgh, Scotland on April 21, 1865, the son of John and Mary Curran Ward of Edinburgh. Peter and his family ended up moving to Wolfe Island, Canada in 1883 when he was eighteen.[3] Later, Peter Ward married Margaret Laughlin, also of Canada. In 1889, the couple moved to Watertown, New York and lived at 602 Mill Street for a while, and eventually moved to 107 East Lynde Street, the same house in which my brother Bill and his family would later reside.

Grandpa Ward operated a small grocery store on the corner of Mill and East Lynde Street; a brick building that still stands there today.[4] The store was a source of all kinds of sugar goodies for the neighborhood kids and I wonder if Grandpa really made much money on this endeavor. Because he was such a strong Christian and so quick to help those in need, one could guess that he probably gave away more than he sold.

Grandpa's nephew John Ward also resided with him. John was the son of Peter and Margaret Ward. Another visitor to Grandpa Ward's house was his own sister Margaret Ward (Maggie). Maggie was born in Belfast Ireland around 1878. She came to the United States on two separate occasions and stayed here on her last visit in 1913. On September 26, 1920, Maggie disappeared and was later found dead. It was rumored that she was desperately

---

[3] It's interesting to note that Grandpa Ward came to Wolfe Island one year after Wilson Ambrose; my father's father arrived there.
[4] My granddaughter Makayla's mother currently runs her beauty salon business from this same building.

despondent on being away from her beloved Ireland and took her own life.

Our Grandpa Ward died in July 1949. When our family speaks of him today, it is always with much respect for the way he lived his life. Personally, when I think of him, I remember so well the little black change purse he would take out of his pocket, open up and hand out coins to us kids. This habit of his also results in a memory I am not too proud of.

I had been anticipating our weekly visit with him one day because I knew it would result in receiving some money to buy bubble gum. Bubble gum was so in demand during the War that it would be sold out of the stores on the same day it arrived. Rationing of certain products because the ingredients were greatly needed to fight the war effort was something we learned to live with. However, I never could figure out why the soldiers needed my gum to fight the Japanese, but by God if it helped in any way, I was more than happy to give up chewing for a while. I reasoned that maybe because of the toughness of the gum, it was used for rubber for their Army trucks. The war was on when I was four and five years old, and at that age, no one bothers explaining much to you. I just learned that sugar, gum, butter and a whole lot of other good stuff was rationed and not available very often. But the war was over now and I was looking forward to getting some money and buying as much Fleer's Double Bubble Gum as my mouth would hold.

As Grandpa slowly took out his worn change purse that day and opened the silver clasps, I was standing very close to him and breathing in what we all recognized as his "Grandpa Ward" smell. It wasn't offensive; a little mixture of tobacco, his well worn dark blue suit and some skunky smelling shaving cream. But it was a smell I can conjure up as I write these words today.

On this particular day I was hoping he might even spring for a quarter (unheard of in those days from any kid that lived on the north side of Mill Street bridge), but who knew? But Grandpa only dolled out two pennies to me and the same to my sister Margaret. I remember telling him in what I thought was a sweet little voice "Oh, that's not very much, you can keep it." Wrong! One look in his eyes told me that I had hurt him deeply. But he smiled at me and patted my hand while in the background, Mom yelled "Katherine!" She was embarrassed, Grandpa was hurt and I was humiliated. I remember going up to the bathroom and tears just started pouring from my eyes. I had never meant to hurt him because I loved him so much. But it was too late. I did try to make it up to him after that. If he gave me as much as five pennies, I acted like he had given me his pension check. Some lessons are learned hard.

    The best gift Grandpa Ward gave my mother was her religious fervor, a fervor that did not leave her all the 95 years of her life. She received that gift from witnessing Grandpa go out of his way to help anyone in need, and in general, just living his life the way God intended us all to live.

    Grandpa walked to morning Mass at Our Lady of the Sacred Heart Church almost every day of his life. And when he got there, he took time to shovel the entranceway to the church in the winter. And on his way home after services, he could be seen shoveling the walkways and driveways of those too ill to take care of it themselves. Everyone knew "Pete" Ward as a man of character and kindness.

    As a young girl growing up and living with Grandpa, Mom enjoyed spending weekends with her many girlfriends. She and these friends worked in several of the local stores in downtown Watertown, mostly as clerks at places like the Fanny Farmer's candy store on Public Square. Mom loved to recall spending weekends at Thompson Park with her girlfriends, where they would share sandwiches and play games together. Having seen photos of the long, bustled dresses that she and they wore back then, it's hard to imagine being able to be involved in anything much more strenuous than croquet. Later, as a married woman with her own children, Mom would often suggest that our family should all go up to Thompson Park for our family get-togethers. However, once we had our own families, we usually opted for the more popular beach locations such as Westcott's or Southwick's where our children could play in the water. But because of Mom's strong memories of fun-filled days as a young girl at the Park, it remained a sentimental favorite to her.

Mary C. Taylor
(Mom)

1918 –
18 years old

Ambrose W. Taylor
(Dad)

US Army Soldier –
WW1

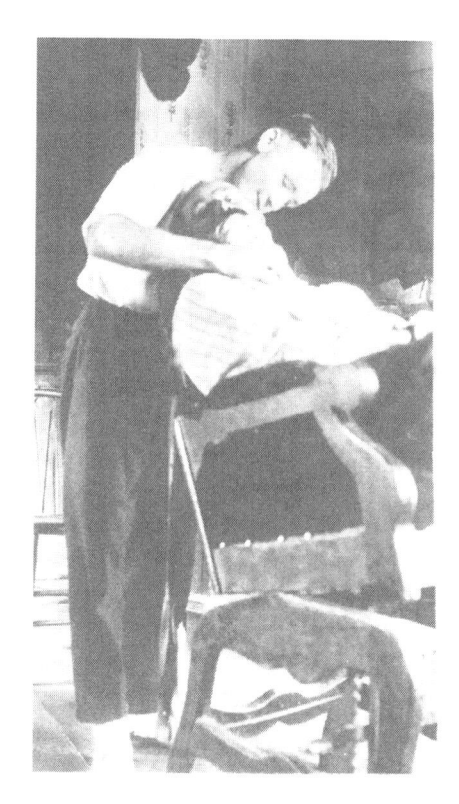

"Dad the Barber"

(Blacksmiths, like Dad, were allowed to perform as barbers)

1920's

Peter Ward "Grandpa"

Out back of his E. Lynde St. Home

(Later my brother Bill & his family lived here)

Ambrose Taylor – 1914

22 years old and unmarried

Ambrose Taylor – 1920
Still unmarried at 28

"Fiddling" around with a pretty young girl.

This is my very favorite photo of Dad.

15

Mom and Dad with Dad's Canadian Family at their homestead in Wolfe Island

Rear, L to R – Mom, Dad's Mother Catherine Taylor, Aunt Lilly and Aunt Kathleen (Dad's sisters)

Front – Dad holding firstborn Harvey.
Dorothy and Mary Baker,
Uncle Frank (Aunt Lilly's husband),
Eileen Baker, Ambrose Doyle)

Mom was pregnant with Jack

Chapter 2

They Met, They Married and They Moved!

"Mr. Postman, may I have another Change of Address Card, Please?"

My father was born Ambrose William Taylor on January 4, 1892, a son of Wilson and Catherine Taylor.[5] My grandfather Wilson Taylor owned a blacksmith shop that was located down the street from his home in Marysville, Ontario, Canada. My father later took up the same profession and was a blacksmith in the Canadian Army during the First World War. He retuned home to Marysville in 1918 and then moved to Rochester, NY. A few years later, he became a US citizen and settled in Deferiet, New York.

Mom met my father during a train trip to visit her girlfriends in Rochester. She and another one of her friends would often make this trip during the weekend. On one such trip, Mom spotted a dashing looking man seated a few rows ahead of her in the club car. She admired his looks but was much too shy to make her interest known. A few trips later, this young man sat closer to Mom and it was apparent that he definitely noticed her. He most likely was taken in by her long brown hair, deep-set blue eyes and her shy disposition. Being outwardly forward was not a trait that men admired in the early 1900's.

Ambrose struck up a conversation with the now interested Mary and he was able to find out

---

[5] I was named after my grandmother and my birth certificate spells my first name with a "C". As a teenager, I decided that I liked the looks of a "K" instead and had it legally changed. Now as an adult and realizing the importance of our heritage, I wish I had not done so.

where she lived and worked and why she so often took this particular train. It wasn't long afterwards that they started dating.

Many years later while Mom was in a nursing home, I visited her with pad and pen in hand. I told her I would like to "interview" her as I wanted to know more about her life as a young girl and how she met my father. I was in the process at the time of filling in the pages of a book that I would be giving to my daughter Lisa as a gift. The book was set up with pre-formed questions and all it required was for someone to fill in the answers. The questions asked about the person's youth, school years, dating years, their wedding day, having children, etc. When filled in, it becomes a nice, albeit short, past history of a parent for their child.

Settling in to fill out this book, I sat next to Mom's chair and began the interview which was more like an inquisition as far as she was concerned.

"So Mom," I began, "I want you to tell me a little bit about your years growing up, how you met Dad and when and where you got married."

"Now, why do you want to know all that?" she asked.

"Because you never talk very much about those days and I want my kids to know more about their grandparents."

"Well all right. What do you want to know about me?"

"Well, for example I'd like to know more about what you thought about Dad when you met him. You said he was nice looking but there must have been something more to it than that?"

She thought about that for a few seconds and then replied,

"Well, he seemed very nice and he was very handsome and had a friendly smile. I guess he interested me. We exchanged information and we

🎁 A gift for you

Merry Christmas. Hope you enjoy my little story. Love, Kathy

amazon.com

SDVMygQTwb

Order of December 20, 2015

Qty.	Item
1	Crepe Paper Memories Doe, Katherine Taylor --- Paperback (** P-1-B230C125 **) 1425102891

Return or replace your item
Visit Amazon.com/returns

43/DVMygQTwb/-1 of 1-//UPS-PHLPA-T/
second/7113779/1222-15:00/1222-12:55

B2A

amazon Gift Receipt

Send a Thank You Note

You can learn more about your gift or start a return here too.

Scan using the Amazon app or visit **http://a.co/7bpbDn2**

Crepe Paper Memories
Order ID: 103-3875950-7689063   Ordered on December 20, 2015

began dating and then we got married. That's about it."

So with that, she related to me the one-year courtship she had with Dad in about four sentences. I knew there must be a lot more so I plodded on for another thirty minutes.

It became apparent that this dashing dark-haired man Ambrose and the long brunette haired, demure Mary were a pretty good fit if you believe that opposites attract. Dad was very outgoing, fun loving and had certainly dated a great deal before discovering Mom.

My sister Olga has an album that holds many photos of our father before he had even met Mom. In one photo, he is pulling a pretty young girl in a small wagon. She seems delighted to be with the smiling young man. My favorite one however, shows Dad playing a ukulele while reposing in the arms of an attractive young miss. A ukulele? Who knew? I never even heard him play a kazoo! Perhaps it was a prop and he was making believe he could actually play it. He definitely was showing off for her. That's most likely why she, and a lot of other gals, seemed so enamored of Ambrose. He was a cut-up and a playboy so shouldn't it be a surprise that he would end up with the quiet and religious Mary Ward?

It needs to be pointed out that in the early 1920's, the era may have later been dubbed "The Roaring 20's" because of the rather loose attitude that prevailed, but any decent man of good breeding and religious background would never end up marrying any floozy or girl of questionable habits. So when Ambrose laid eyes of this decently shy woman who showed interest in him, he was probably pretty interested in her by the time the train pulled into the next station.

Most likely after discovering that there was no boyfriend in the wings, just a few giddy girlfriends who enjoyed their weekly trips to the big city for lunch and shopping, Ambrose "went in for the kill." Having heard stories about him from my older siblings and other people who knew Dad better than I ever did, I'm sure Mom fell head over heels.

Eventually they married in Albany, NY at St. Cecelia's Church when Mom was 23 years old and Dad was 31. His age at the time of their marriage gives credence to the fact that Ambrose Taylor had a lot of 'oat-sowing' to get out of his system before he was ready to settle down.

It was said that my Grandpa Ward was not so fond of the young Ambrose Taylor. He probably did not appear good enough for Peter Ward's darling Mary whom he thought of as his very own daughter. This might have been the reason my parents decided to get married out of town.

After their marriage, Mom and Dad settled in Watertown, New York and Dad worked in nearby Deferiet at the St. Regis Papermill, later known as Champion International. The mill became a place where many of my relatives ended up working. During the difficult days of the depression in the late 20's and early 30's, the paper mill kept plugging along and so several of my brothers and my cousins from Deferiet managed to draw a hard earned paycheck each week. My father's sister Lilly Taylor married Francis Baker and he too settled his family in Deferiet. A few of their children worked at the mill for many years; our cousin Eileen retiring from a good position in the front office.

Mom and Dad had ten children in rather rapid succession. Large families were the norm years ago and Mom gave birth every few years in keeping with this trend. My brother Harvey Edward was the first-born. He was followed by John Frederick whom we always called "Jack" and then Olga Marie, followed by William Ambrose, "Bill," then James Patrick, "Jim," Vernon Francis, "Vern," Thomas Leo "Tom," Kathleen Dorothy who died at the age of six months from pneumonia, and finally Margaret Ann and myself, Katherine Louise, "the baby of the family," a title I would own for the rest of my life.

Mom would more often that not introduce me to her friends in this manner. "Katherine, this is Mrs. Mason, and Mrs. Mason, this is my daughter Katherine, the baby of the family." I think when I was real young I believed my full name was "Katherine, The Baby of the Family." It was as if I were the period at the end of Mom's life sentence of delivering babies.

When I was only six weeks old, Mom decided she could not handle Ambrose Taylor's drinking any more so they separated; Dad moving into the Deferiet Hotel so he could be close to his job, and Mom staying pretty much in the Watertown area but managing to change addresses every year or so for most of her life. I think the longest she ever stayed in one place was when she was in the nursing home in her later years.

For decades we laughingly related stories about coming home from school only to find Mom packing up the moving truck to move us to another rented apartment. Sometimes the new home was but a block or two away. The excuses were varied but always had the same underlining theme of sudden dissatisfaction with the current rental. There have been estimates that she moved more than thirty times, a number that may very well be too low. The frequent moves didn't bother me until I became a teenager and realized that my friends did not move every year or so. In fact, most of them were in the same homes in 8th grade that they were in when in Kindergarten; a statistic that shocked me when I learned of it.

As an adult relating the story of our family's many moves to acquaintances, I have been often asked if it was difficult to constantly be in so many new schools. I have always answered that it was indeed hard at times because attending a new school is rarely without some sort of emotional fear. You as the "new kid on the block" are subject to scrutiny when walking into class for the first time. It's a lucky child that only has to endure that once or twice in their lifetime.

I recall my first day back at Holy Family School for 8th grade. I say "back" because I had attended that school while in 5th grade and then after a couple of years in schools on the north side of town, we moved close to Holy Family again. Once more I had to face a first day as the "new kid." The result was that when I awoke that morning, I was so filled with fear that I lost my voice and could not speak a word when Mom and I met up with the school Principal in her office.

"Welcome back, Katherine," Sister Anna Marie said. "Are you anxious to meet up with some of your old friends again?"

I just nodded my head up and down and tried to sit on my shaking hands. How could I explain to her that I was petrified of re-entering this school in the middle of the semester, wondering if my old classmates would remember me? Would they accept me like an old long, lost friend or just ignore me?

I don't remember too much about entering the classroom. I most likely took the first seat I could find near the door and tried to not look conspicuous. That was my usual "M.O." when entering a new school. However, I do remember that about an hour into the class, our teacher Sister Daniel asked questions randomly of students from a history book. I was shocked when she asked me. I thought she might leave me alone until I felt more comfortable. But why I remember this so clearly is because the question was one that I knew the answer to, as we had already covered that subject at Sacred Heart School, the school I had just transferred from! How lucky was this?

So now I was dying to answer it and it appeared that everyone was waiting to see how dumb or smart I was. Sister didn't know that I had laryngitis and so she waited for me to say something. The question in the book had three possible answers listed in three numbered paragraphs. I knew that the second answer was the correct one so I held up two fingers to answer. It was correct and so she said aloud "That's right Katherine, number two is the correct answer because....." She went on to discuss the question and answer and suddenly I knew I had my voice back. I could now relax and be myself.

By the end of the school day, I was eager to come back to school the next day with my new (old) friends. I had overcome that challenge once again. To this day, I'm not afraid to enter a room full of strangers and begin to mingle with them. No doubt because of this unasked-for gift given to me by my mother, "Gypsy Mary."

Watertown had four local Catholic schools and with the exception of St. Anthony's school in the Italian section of Watertown, I attended the others not only once, but several times. I began first grade at Our Lady of the Sacred Heart School. There was no Kindergarten at the time so once you turned five or six, you began school. I remember loving school and especially Spelling Bees. Having been born with a competitive nature, these competitions allowed me to try to outsmart my fellow classmates with something I was rather good at.

My teacher, who usually was a Sister of St. Joseph, would ask us to line up along the two sides of the classroom. She would throw out a word for a student to spell, and if successful, the student would remain standing. Once the student failed, they were disqualified and had to sit down. The last student remaining was the Spelling Bee Champion for the day. I remember asking poor Sister Georgina on a daily basis if we could have another spelldown. If I wasn't the winner, I was at least one of the last two or three standing and I found the competition to be very rewarding.

Classrooms in the 1940's were divided into *A* and *B* groups. Those students who excelled were placed in the *A* group and the others remained in the *B* group. The first grade classroom had four rows of seats and the rows were divided by these groups. Interestingly, I discovered that the smarter group of kids was placed closer to the blackboard and were often asked to stay after school and erase the blackboards and then clean the erasers. Obviously, I reasoned, only a real smart kid could figure out how to make chalk disappear. (I had been placed in the *B* group, much to my dismay).

For whatever reason, I longed to clean those boards and I realized this meant getting into the proper row of seats. In addition to wanting to be responsible for getting rid of the daily chalked-up mangle of words and numbers on the blackboard, I also decided that I wanted to be in the group with Monica, the pretty brunette who had impeccable manners and seemed super-smart, and Anthony, who was so cute and also just seemed to know everything. But the problem was that I didn't know how one got into the *A* group. It seemed to me that something that a student did or said; perhaps the right answer to a question may have been the catalyst that advanced you. All I knew was that I had to be in the *A* student row. That blackboard was calling me!

Soon it became obvious to me that it was all about convincing Sister you were smarter than many of the other students. My opportunity came on the day that the *B* group I was in was told to read a chapter in our *Dick and Jane* primer while the *A* group were to work on the series of words that Sister printed on the blackboard. Surprisingly, many of the printed words on the board seemed to be sticklers for them. I remember the word *pencil* and *purple* being up there and not one of the A group kids knew it, but I did! Would I dare to possibly incur Sister's wrath by yelling out the answer? I was too afraid to do that so when it became obvious that none of the A group kids was going to answer, I raised my hand into the air, first shyly and then waving it somewhat reminiscent of a Queen waving to her adoring subjects from a balcony.

"Katherine, do you have to go to the basement?" she asked me. Not an unusual question for me as I was always taking trips to the bathroom, which in this school was always referred to as "the basement".

Embarrassed but willing to take the challenge and be bold, I stood up and said,

"Sister, I know what those two words are." She looked at me for a few seconds and then said, "Well then dear, why don't you read them for us."

"They're *purple* and *pencil*, Sister," I said and then sat back down, a very sheepish grin planted squarely on my face. Anthony looked at me and smiled and Monica appeared a little shocked. After all, I was not in the more elite A group to which she belonged. How could *I* possibly know these words?

Sister thanked me, wrote something in her little black book which was located on the right hand side of her tidy oak desk, and the very next day of school, my seat was moved to the A group. I wasn't just happy, I was ecstatic! And to make things even more perfect, after school I was asked to clean the blackboard and then take the erasers outside to clap them against the brick wall of the school. I may need to visit a psychiatrist to figure out why I could not get the big grin off my face as I clapped those erasers so hard that white dust was all over my clothes and hair. I was in "brown-nose" heaven.

Sadly that experience of happiness was quickly overshadowed a few days later by the "bathroom break" fiasco.

I think I had the weakest bladder in the history of any first grader. This, along with the fact that a student anxious to use the restroom had to try to get a busy teacher's attention before being excused, could be a challenge. First you had to raise your hand and ask and receive permission (as long as it appeared you did not just want to roam the halls). This could take anywhere from thirty incredibly long seconds to a full minute if Sister was otherwise preoccupied. On the day of my bathroom break dilemma, the urge to "go" was instant and powerful. Sister was facing the blackboard. She was fervently adding some new words that we would have to learn. As excited as I was about the new word challenge, and thinking that if really, really lucky, we might have a Spelling Bee that day, my kidneys were of the utmost importance right then.

Sister was taking too long. My legs were crossed; my fingers were crossed and eventually so were my eyes. When I finally got Sister's attention, it was too late – way too late. I could feel the warm water edging out of my winter bloomers (a staple in our home during the colder weather) and then puddling beneath my desk. The boy in front of me named Donnie, heard or felt what was taking place. He turned towards me and seeing the look of embarrassment on my face, yelled out loud "Oh my gosh, Katherine just peed her pants!" Thank you, Donnie.

Sister quickly moved to my side, took my hand and led me from the classroom. The back of my little red and black wool plaid skirt, (handed down from my sister Margaret) was thankfully sopping up the majority of the urine. Donnie's snickers could be heard as Sister and I walked to the nurse's office two doors away.

The shelves in our school nurse's office held all sorts of medical necessities; band-aids, thermometers, combs for hair-lice extermination and other goodies. They also held woolen bloomers of varying sizes that were even more bulky and disgusting looking than the ones I was wearing.

Sister left in me in the nurse's capable hands and went back to our classroom which by now was getting completely out of hand. For the teacher to leave the room even for a couple of minutes was cause for instant chatter and bedlam and I *knew* they were all discussing this very funny incident that happened, thank God not to them, but to me. I planned on never looking at Anthony in the face again. And Monica was probably laughing hysterically right along with Donnie. The little twit!

It only took a minute for me to change from one ugly pair of pink bloomers to the cleaner, dryer multi-flowered pair handed to me by the sympathetic school nurse. She then advised me I could return to my class, leaving my old pair of underpants in her possession. Obviously it was used as a trade-in...you left your old wet ones there, took a clean pair, the old pair got washed and dried and took its place on the shelf waiting for the next weak-bladdered kid.

Now if you think I had already endured the worst part of the day, you would be wrong. I took a deep breath as I turned the doorknob, opened it and headed for my seat. But wait – what was going on here? On his hands and knees, wiping up the puddle from underneath my desk with a bunch of old rags, was a very angry Donnie. Obviously Sister felt that as long as he thought this was so funny, he could have the honor of cleaning up the "accident." If she felt this would make me feel better, she could not have been more wrong!

Walking home from school that day, I slithered behind every tree and bush I could find;

positive that at any moment Donnie would lunge out and kill me for his acute embarrassment. But kids at that age forget things quickly and it only took about a half of a semester before I could look at him again.

    I see good old Donnie locally from time to time in social situations or in stores or restaurants. I am always one insane instant away from asking him if he remembers the incident. I figure that if he does remember, every time he looks at me, he is thinking "There's Katherine, the pants-wetter." Therefore he already knows that about me and wouldn't it be better just to bring it up and laugh about it now that we both have grandchildren who might be in the same situation? But then again, perhaps what happened to Donnie *after* the incident was more traumatic to him than it was to me and therefore he remembers nothing. At least I hope so. So I've kept my mouth shut.

    Our family habit of moving so often obviously did not escape its having a strong impression on my psyche. I knew in high school that it made me sad to so often have to tell my friends and teachers that I had a new address.

    So it's not surprising that years later, when an adult with my own children, I was faced with how much the frequent moves had really made its impact on me.

    It was Christmas time and I was seated on the floor of our Cooper Street home in front of the television set, wrapping gifts. The TV show that was on that moment dealt with a pop psychiatrist instructing viewers on how to go back to childhood days and deal with our "inner child," correcting any problems that may have caused us a lot of grief. I was finding it mildly amusing until he told viewers to close our eyes and go back to being about 7 or 8 years of age, to see ourselves walking in our front door, to travel in our minds up the stairs and into our bedrooms and lie on our bed. Being bored with the idea of still having to wrap the many presents I had in front of me, I decided to play along and so I closed my eyes.

As instructed, I began mentally looking for the door to my childhood home. But what door? The one that opens the house in Herrings?, Black River?, Carthage?, in Watertown, NY on High Street?, North Hamilton?, Hancock Street?, Grant Street?, Gale Street?, Stuart Street? (we lived on that street twice), Mill Street?, Bronson Street?, Summer Street?, Pearl Street Road?, William Street? (lived there twice), South Massey Street?, North Orchard Street?, East Hills Apartments?, West Lynde Street?, West Main Street?, Phelps Street?, Curtis Street?, Boyd Street, North Rutland Street? (lived there twice)? Which front door? He was going too fast. "Slow Down!" I shouted at the television set. "Let me think of a house first"!

Quickly, I settled on the house on Stuart Street, figuring that because it was one of the very same houses that I lived in on two separate occasions, I might have a better memory of it. The TV shrink was now instructing us to look at our bed covers, our curtains, the room's color scheme, our safe environment. But I *couldn't* settle on a color because each of the dozen or so bedrooms had different windows, different beds, and a different color scheme. I use the words "color scheme" loosely, as most of the time it was whatever chenille bedspread had survived a hundred tub washings over the past ten or so years. Mom was nothing if not frugal.

Not being able to settle on anything familiar or comforting, I was so frustrated that hovering over the packages of red and green Christmas bows, I started sobbing like a baby. I couldn't remember anything like the audience members were able to and it made me so sad.

Today I can look back at all these moves and laugh about it, wondering what in the world Mom was thinking when she'd have to pack up boxes for the umpteenth time that year, instruct all us kids to gather our belongings and be ready to move to a "much nicer," "much warmer," "much larger," "much cheaper," (take your pick) place. For a couple of these moves, my brothers would even walk down the road with beds on their backs, moving them to a new house located perhaps just around the corner. The neighbors would hardly offer us a glance.

It was more like, "Hi Mary, moving again I see?"

"Yes, Beatrice, the kids and I are moving to a nicer house around the corner."

"Oh, that will be nice, Mary."

"Yes, it will be cheaper in the winter. We're supposed to have a cold one and the furnace where we are now is too old."

What kind of furnace the new house would have was the number one reason for moving. Mom probably could have gone into the furnace repair business if she had the desire. She could tell you how much coal you'd need for a winter just by taking a look at the size of the monstrous belly of the beast.

The rent she would be paying was the number two reason for the move. Sometimes the subject of rent would be an exciting subject for Mom to talk about but could prove embarrassing for me.

When I was a senior in high school, I dated a fellow for a few months who was attending Georgetown University. His family came from money and lived in a beautiful house on the other side of town. As a rule, when I would date anyone of his caliber, I usually tried to make arrangements to meet them somewhere so they wouldn't have to see where we lived or even worse, see the boxes that were piled up in the living room, waiting to be unpacked or packed, depending on whether we had just moved or were getting ready to.

I met Frank more or less on a blind date and we double dated with my friend Marilyn and her boyfriend. After a night that included a trip to a burger stand, Frank insisted on driving me home. I was hoping he would just drop me off and leave but he was too well mannered to do anything like that. He insisted on walking me to the door and perhaps, he asked, could he come in for a minute? I'm thinking: *If you do, I hope Mom is fast asleep.* It would just make things so much easier.

When we entered the house, Mom was wide awake and busy in the living room, unpacking some boxes from our latest move. Clothes were piled up on the couch, newspapers on the floor, her newly washed "snuggies" (the warm, woolen underpants that came in white or pink that Mom favored for warmth and not unlike the "bloomers" we kids wore), draped over the lamp to hasten their drying and everything else in pure disarray. I'm thinking: *Oh no, this has all the earmarks of a disaster.*

I introduced Frank to her and because Frank was so wonderfully mannered, Mom took an instant liking to him and began telling him how we had just moved from a house that had been so cold and drafty and how this one was so much warmer, etc. Frank looked around and told Mom it was a "nice house" and proceeded to make small talk with her. I looked around the living room trying to see it through Frank's eyes, but for the umpteenth time in my life, faced the reality that this one too was *not* that nice of a house. Our furniture was mostly old with the exception of a new rocker or end table that Mom had managed to buy, thanks to scrounging a few bucks from my father. The paint on the wall was a putrid green and the linoleum on the floor was old with frayed edges. I stood there looking at the whole picture, realizing that his house was most likely such a far cry from ours. I'm quietly praying Mom won't get into finances with him like she often did with anyone who would listen. But no such luck.

After Frank made that mistake of telling her the house was nice, Mom shared with him how she had gotten a real bargain.

"I talked the landlord down to $14.50 a month when he had been asking $18.50," she proudly offered.

Frank smiled and complimented Mom on her great deal. I wanted the floor to open up, but damn, it didn't and I stood there red-faced while this wonderful guy told her that she certainly was a lucky woman to get such a bargain and agreed that indeed it would be a nice, warm apartment this coming winter.

Frank went on to college, I went on to other things but I have thought of him a few times since that day. I figure that some gal ended up with a very nice rich guy that never put down the lower class people of the world.

Unfortunately, that was what we were – people of the *lower* class. Not *poor* mind you, but definitely not well off enough to be considered the *middle class*. Years later when I was married and had a pretty decent life, I realized that I now was considered middle class in the pecking order of society. It was then that I knew even if we were probably considered lower class when I was young, almost everyone else I cared about was too. We didn't much worry about the societal ladder, because how we were treated, how much fun we had and how close our family was, were the important things about life. Mom did a great job making us feel "*upper class.*"

The houses that we quickly moved to, inhabited for a year, or if lucky more, always looked better after Mom did what she could to brighten it up. Mom hated dark colors of any kind, so once she re-painted a few walls a lighter color, hung up frilly bright colored curtains; it took on the feeling of home. And she loved to bake her famous rolls and biscuits, so entering the house after school and smelling that wonderful odor of fresh baked rolls made the house seem warm and inviting. One could even overlook the air-drying snuggies.

The scariest sight upon entering would be if you caught Mom scanning the classified apartment rental section of the newspaper. Always with a smile on her face. "Oh, look at this place, three bedrooms, big backyard, and brand new furnace." Oh no, here we go again!

These frequent house moves always made Mom smile a lot. She enjoyed the change, the settling in, the arranging of our meager furniture in rooms of an unfamiliar layout, against a different, if not sadly faded, flower-patterned wallpaper. When I became an adult, I had a new insight about these moves. I truly think that Mom was always moving from place to place, almost as a way to find her roots; looking figuratively to find out where she came from. Of course she obviously failed at this because she sure kept the moving van companies in business for the rest of her life.

When we made the move to William Street during the time I attended 8th grade at Holy Family School, I came home about the second week of school to discover movers carrying our furniture around the walk at the side of the house and to the apartment at the rear of that very same building. It was "warmer back there," I remember her telling us. When I went back to school the next day, I told my teacher that I was in error when I originally told her my family lived at 131 William Street. I corrected her and gave her the new address of 129 William Street.

"Sorry about the error Sister," I told her. I figured that it was easier to just tell her that, rather than try to explain that I was the youngest child of a nomad.

If all this was not normal, we didn't really realize it until much later. I can clearly remember as a young girl being in the house with my brother Tom when Mom came home to tell us she had been talking to a woman who could foresee the future. Mom certainly never believed in psychics as they were *from the devil*, but this woman she told us, was very religious and had a "gift from God"; a huge difference to Mom.

Tom excitedly asked Mom what the woman had told her and Mom replied that the woman informed her that we would all be moving to a new house within the year. I remember Tom laughing so hard and telling Mom that *anyone* knew that about the Taylor's. I don't think Mom was too happy with his reply, but even in his youth, Tom had it figured out pretty well.

Anyway, I think it was around the time of my watching the TV shrink as an adult that I decided I would not move from our home until our kids were grown. I always wanted them to remember the same entrance door to the house, the same door to their bedroom and the layout of their room. I wanted them to have that because it was so missing in my life.

That was obviously a good decision because when in 1999 we sold our Cooper Street home that we lived in since 1960, our kids told us that they would so miss that house with all its many memories. They felt an attachment to it and that gave them security. I know they never had to stop and think about which house they would be entering when school was out. And I know they will always be able to picture the front door when they close their eyes and try to conjure up memories. I find comfort in knowing that their father and I provided that for them.

In fact when the house was completely empty but we had not yet handed over the keys to the new owners, my son Michael used his own key to enter the house and was sad when he found the telephone had already been disconnected. He later told me that he had wanted to phone his brother Rick and do a walk-through of the house, remembering all the good times in it.

At the time, Rick was living in Massachusetts and Mike said he wanted to say to him, "*Hey Rick, I'm now walking into our old bedroom. Remember when we were kids and we would lay here on Christmas morning waiting for Mom and Dad to tell us we could come downstairs...that Santa had come so it was now okay? And how we'd run so fast and hard that we'd knock each other over trying to get down first?*"

And he wanted to say to him, "*I'm looking out into the back yard now. Remember when we used to do our Evil Kneivel daredevil stunts out there? We'd make a ramp and get our old bikes and drive them like mad and see how high we could fly in the air off the ramp?*"

Even though he was sad that couldn't call him, it was really okay. All our kids have wonderful memories that they will be able to conjure up at a moment's notice when, as older parents, they find themselves cross-legged in front of their television sets, wrapping their kid's Christmas presents. When the current TV shrink asks them to take themselves back to their youth, to the comfort of their bedrooms and remember the walls, their beds, their color schemes, they'll have no problems. Maybe staying in one house for so long can be seen as boring to some people, but to those who would have given their right arm for that privilege, it's priceless.

That being said, it needs to be told that having a mother who had a lust for wandering did not make for a life of sadness. Being the youngest of nine children offered many opportunities for fun and frolic. Mom did all she could to make sure we were well fed and had fun times. I'm sure it was very hard for her to keep everything going with no husband in the house to help out. She worked at as many jobs as she had houses. She worked behind the soda fountain in a drug store, in a candy store as a cashier, was a housekeeper, a laundress and a babysitter for people who had spoiled little rich kids and needed a nanny. I remember being with her one time while she cooked for a few days for wealthy people who were on vacation. The child in the home was about my age, ten or so, and when Mom told her she could call her "Mrs. Taylor," the obnoxious brat replied "I'll call you '*Cook*'." I remember Mom not being too happy about that one but it was all about the paycheck, providing a roof over our head and food on the table that allowed her to take some jobs that were certainly humiliating to her.

Dad did his best to help us out. He made monthly visits to the house, expecting to see us and give Mom some money but usually finding us not there. Mom loved to pack us all on the public bus and head downtown to shop or visit one of her friends. I think I was about ten or so when I realized that not having a father in the house all the time was not the norm. Divorce was nowhere near as prevalent as today and Mom certainly wasn't about to get one of "those" – forbidden by the Catholic Church at the time. So she told everyone that she and my father were *separated* and used that term until Dad died at age 60 of cancer. After that, she was a *widow*.

I think any child who belongs to a low-income family realizes it when the first big event in their life comes along, like a dance or birthday party or the like, and the money may not be there. For me it was when I was in 8th grade and the Principal gave me a note one day to take home to Mom. Being curious, probably *nosy* is a better word, I opened it up as soon as I was off the school grounds and read its contents. It was a plea for Mom to pay the school some money owed; whether tuition or for books I don't remember. I'm sure keeping all the bills paid was difficult for a single woman with meager earnings and at least four children still at home.

    The next day, Mom took me to the pastor of Holy Family Church. I remember him as being very kind and quite young. After listening to Mom's plea and his hearing that she was a woman without a husband and trying to give her poor little kids a decent Catholic education, he handed her a voucher that not only took care of the delinquent bill but was also good at a grocery street on High Street. At that time we were living on William Street and I was able to take this piece of paper to the store, pick up bread and milk as instructed by Mom, and we wouldn't have to pay a dime! Man, I thought that was pretty neat. I realized much later that it was similar to Welfare, something I suspect Mom was not too proud to have to accept. But she did what she had to do for her kids and that was that. Besides there was a lot to be said for being able to buy a package of Necco candies with only a piece of paper signed by the church pastor.

    At one point in my school-hopping young life, Margaret and I believed we would be attending school in Carthage, NY instead Watertown. It was during the summer before I was to enter 8th grade that Mom informed us that we would be moving to Carthage because she had taken a job at the St. James Church rectory as a cook. So Margaret and I said goodbye to all our school chums, packed up our belongings and off we went to live in the upstairs apartment over the rectory. The one good thing about the move was that two young teenage girls hitting a town as small as Carthage gave us the opportunity to be 'the new girls in town'. As soon as we unpacked our few belongings, we hit the streets checking out the town. There was a soda fountain downtown and that, we discovered, was the main gathering place for the area teenagers. We quickly scoped out the boys and within a week we had a couple of them hanging around the rectory, (our new home, after all), much to the chagrin of the priests.

Ronnie, the boy I liked, happened to be an altar boy and consequently had to enter the cook's quarters (now my mother's quarters) to retrieve the wine from the refrigerator each morning. The wine of course was used by the priests to be sanctified during the Mass. I think this was the only summer of my young life when I was out of bed before eight o'clock in order to get to greet Ronnie on his rounds.

But alas, as our young love lives were just getting off the ground, Mom decided that these particular priests were too fussy and so we moved back home. From which house we moved to Carthage and to which house we returned, is something my mind has blanked out. A mind can only retain so many packings and unpackings before they all blur into one.

First 6 Taylor Kids – Deferiet, NY – 1933
Front - Olga, Bill, Vern and Jim
Rear – Harvey and Jack   (Mom, pregnant with Tom can barely be seen on porch right)

Mom and Dad with their first 7 children - 1934
Bill, Olga, Harvey, Jack, Vern, Jim, & Dad holding Tom
Mom was pregnant with Kathleen who later died.

Chapter 3

Siblings

"Quit your crying or I'll give you something to cry about!"

    We may have moved a lot; money may have been in short supply, but the Taylor clan was a pretty decent bunch and we had a lot of laughs growing up. My brothers were characters for sure and they kept us in stitches. My brother Vern possessed the meanest streak (maybe *sadistic* is a better term) as far as Margaret and I were concerned. He lived to make our lives pure Hell. Of course we didn't know that this was just his way; he was full of mischief and had tons of energy. We just knew that he was a real thorn in our sides.
    When we lived on Grant Street, our upstairs bathroom was unfinished for some reason. Perhaps it was being remodeled or just never finished off, but the side towards the hall was plywood as opposed to being a solid wood wall. There was a little hole in the plywood just over the toilet paper hangar and you could peek out but (luckily) not in. I was only about six or seven at the time and I remember sitting on the toilet one day when I heard Vernon walk by the outside of the bathroom. On impulse; I stuck my little finger out and waved it at him, calling his name. His answer to that was to try to cut my finger off! Of course, he wasn't really going to, but he pretended to saw it with something that was sharp enough to at least feel like a knife; making a grating noise with his throat, convincing me I would be pulling back a stump. He just constantly tried to make our life miserable.

Vernon realized at a real young age that he could scare the heck out of me, my sister or any of our friends who visited us. He could lay in wait in a closet or behind a door for the longest time, hoping to catch us off guard. He'd jump out, screaming and yelling like a wild animal, sending our friends out the front door in tears. This of course gave him *exactly* the response he was hoping for.

And he could connive with the best of them. I recall a specific incident that will serve as a good example. One night when I was quite young, I was in bed, my head settled on my fluffy pillow, waiting for sleep to take over. Vernon came in to tell me how bad it was for little kids to have their heads up high all night long on a pillow. He lovingly informed me that if I removed the pillow and lay flat, I would have better posture when I grew up. He explained that old people, like Mrs. Donato who lived around the corner and was all humped over, always slept on a pillow. This, he related to me, was the reason she looked like that and he, as my benevolent older brother, would prevent that from ever happening to me.

Suddenly, I so loved this older brother who I realized was graciously looking out for my welfare. I gladly gave him my pillow and tried desperately to sleep on my old, hard bed without one. Only later when I heard Mom yelling at him and demanding that he give me back my pillow and that "he did not need two of them," did I realize that maybe he wasn't such a great brother after all.

But of course he really was and when he joined the Army later on and ended up stationed in Germany, I remember thinking that I might never see him again. It was past wartime but I did not think that made much difference. I was sure an enemy soldier would kill him. I began to long for him to come back home and torment me again. Eventually he returned and for months we had to listen to him speak German. He had picked up more than just a few words and phrases while overseas and I thought it was kind of neat to be able to talk in a different language.

I memorized some German phrases that I would use at school to impress my classmates. The only problem with that is that one of the nuns was of German descent and when I used a particular phrase I had heard Vern use the night before while talking with our brother Tom, Sister called me aside and looked at me sternly and said "Katherine, don't you ever say that again!" Obviously Vern had more in his vocabulary than that which translated to "Attention" "Good Morning," "Darling" and the like.

I'm rather sad to say that when Vern ended up marrying Alice and leaving our house, it was the first time that Margaret and I could go to bed at night without fear of some sort of unknown "attack" taking place. I often wondered if poor Alice had to put up with his scare tactics or did marrying get rid of those demons in him?

Later my brother Jim also joined the army and ended up in Korea. I was a very sympathetic kid during this time. I'd cry at the drop of a hat. When I would write my letters to Jim, I would put a 45 record on the turntable to listen to while I wrote. The song had to be sad; that evoked exactly the kind of emotion I wanted to impart to him. I thought he would love knowing how sad I was without him. In retrospect, it probably was very hard on him to get a letter that told him something to the effect of "I miss you so much and I am listening right now to "*I'll Be Seeing You*"[6] and tears are coming down my eyes while I write this." That sure must have made it easier for him to spend another day in combat!

But most often I'd play my favorite song, "*Over There*," the song written by the great George M. Cohen that became the rallying cry for the soldiers of

---

[6] By Tommy Dorsey and his orchestra

World War II. I could never listen to this song without feeling such a sense of pride for the soldiers who were fighting for our country. This was a war that was supported by all Americans. I could tell that adults felt that it was noble cause, it was worth the blood shed and it was about assuring freedom for the entire world. So I'd put the song on the record player and my chest would expand with pride while I listened to the words sung by Billy Murray about our American troops:

Over There

Over There, Over There
Send the word, send the word over there--
That the Yanks are coming,
The Yanks are coming,
The drums rum-tumming
Ev'rywhere.
So prepare, say a pray'r,
Send the word, send the word to beware.
We'll be over, we're coming over,
And we won't come back till it's over
Over there.

On one occasion I wrote a lengthy letter to Jim while he was in Korea and asked Mom to mail it for me. It was exceptionally long and filled with all kinds of news of the Taylor family. About a month later (mail in those days from overseas took forever to receive), I read his reply in which he told me that he couldn't wait to get to mail call the day my letter arrived. No one had written him lately and when his sergeant called his name to come and get his mail, he was a little upset that there was only one letter but at least he had that one from his little sister, Kate.

He went to a corner in the tent, lit a cigarette and opened my letter. Most likely he was expecting to read another paragraph or two of how sad my life was without him. Instead what the envelope contained was - - nothing! Apparently I had sealed the envelope and mistakenly threw the letter away without even realizing it. Later he wrote to tell me how sad that made him feel and would I please make sure that didn't happen again? After reading that letter from him, I was so upset that I put the song "*PS, I Love You,* written by Johnny Mercer on the phonograph and wrote him twice as much as usual, tears dripping from my eyes.

PS, I Love You

Dear, I thought I'd drop a line
The weather's cool, the folks are fine
I'm in bed each night at nine
(P.S.-I love you)

Yesterday we had some rain
But, all in all, I can't complain
Was it dusty on the train?
(P.S.-I love you)

Write to the Browns just as soon as you're able
They came around to call
I burned a hole in the dining room table
And let me see, I guess that's all

Nothing else for me to say
And so I'll close but, by the way
Everybody's thinking of you
(P.S.-I love you)

I guess you could say I was a sappy little creature in my youth. It's a good thing I was not older during wartime. I'm sure I would have been the type of girl to be next to suicidal if her boyfriend was in combat. God knew what he was doing to have me born early enough and before I had the chance to make a huge fool of myself. Although a few years later I would get an opportunity to write love letters to a guy stationed overseas. But it was during peacetime so all I feared then was that he might get his foot run over by an Army Jeep.

Summer of 1942 –

Margaret (4) &
Katherine (2)

In front of Olga (16)
And Mom (42)

Margaret
and
Katherine

Winter of
1943

5 1/2 and 3
1/2years old.

*I think I look
like my brother
Harvey's
daughter Trudy
here.*

Chapter 4

"Lights, Camera, Action"

"Wait, I've got a tear in my crepe paper costume"

My sister Margaret and I were very imaginative as youngsters and most of all, we loved our weekly backyard plays while living on Stuart Street. These were the days of Judy Garland and Mickey Rooney movies. These young MGM studio stars were famous for their movie plots of gathering up the neighborhood kids and putting on a play for various causes and reasons. If Judy told Mickey that there was a neighborhood kid who needed some money for his sick mother, then the next thing you know, a stage was built, the curtain went up and out came a whole group of kids singing beautifully to a band that was never seen.

The Stuart Street gang took up the cause too. This was right after World War II and the cost of goods was still pretty high so putting on a play that necessitated the girls wearing costumes created a cash flow. I remember hitting up Dad when he'd come for our visits or taking milk bottles back to the Red and White grocery store on Mill Street for the two cent deposit. With the money earned, we'd go to Woolworth's Department Store downtown by city bus or walk the couple of miles if we didn't have the required nickel for a bus token. There, we'd buy crepe paper for our skirts - we *had* to have crepe paper. Red, blue and green were favorites but sometimes we needed white too if the play had a patriotic theme.

Margaret and I and the other girls in the play would crimp the edges of the paper to make scalloped edges. This was a serious project. You'd lay the crepe paper out on a table. Then placing your first and second finger of your right hand in a "V", you'd hold firmly while you crimped scalloped edges through the "V" with the index finger of your other hand. This would take some time but as our plays became more frequent; our talent for designing these skirts became keener. Then we'd gather the finished product around our waist and somehow attach them. These skirts were a thing of beauty in my young mind.

What served as a shirt or blouse to accompany the skirt was anything you could find as long as it was colorful. I recall securing one of Olga's scarves across my boob-less chest once. I'm sure I returned it to her dresser before being discovered. I felt very grownup that day and thought I looked an awful lot like Betty Grable.

We'd make signs and advertise throughout the neighborhood that a play would be held the next day. The songs we chose were from the War era such as the *Boogie Woogie Bugle Boys*, *Over There* and another personal favorite, *Bell Bottom Trousers*. Not having the invisible band behind the stage like Judy and Mickey had, we'd play the records that our friend Jeannette would get from her house and we'd dance to the songs, swishing our little crepe paper skirts. I was never happier than the days of our backyard vaudeville shows.

When we weren't involved in bringing Hollywood and vaudeville to the Stuart Street neighborhood, Margaret and I loved to make mud pies in the backyard. We'd get together with a couple of the girls on the same street and we'd collect red berries and green leaves. If we were lucky and Mom could afford it, she'd let us have a little white flour. We'd mix up some dirt with water, shape the resulting mud into little pies, cover them with the berries and leaves, and sprinkle the flour on top for a sugaring effect. All you needed was a little creativity, as any back yard held all sorts of wonderful pie "ingredients."

Hollyhock dolls were another activity for the girls in the neighborhood. We were lucky enough to have hollyhocks growing out back of our house. They were pretty to look at but became playmates if you had the know-how to turn them into dancing ballerina dolls.

You had to make sure the hollyhock was in full bloom. The petals became the skirt and the doll's head was a peeled bud taken from where the stem had been. You'd invert the flower and shoving it into the stem area, these pretty colored flowers became beautiful dancing dolls. We'd line them up on the stoned wall in the back yard and continue making more until we'd used up all the flowers. Stuart Street was always, in my mind, the place where our creativity was born and nurtured.

I have no doubt that had television been around in the late 40's and early 50's, I never would have been involved in a neighborhood play while wearing homemade crepe paper skirts, or experienced the delight of making playmates from flower blossoms or mud pies that were so real looking they made you drool.

Living on Stuart Street also resulted in an event that I remember so well that to this day, I use it to tease my children and now my children's children. In reading this now, I know my kids are thinking "Oh, no, here comes the *pickle story*." They're right. However, the pickle story begins with our family's penchant for movie-going.

When we were young, Mom loved movies so much that going to the theater downtown to catch the latest Betty Grable or Roy Rogers feature was a weekly event. On many occasions, Mom, my brother Tom, Margaret and I would go to the Avon or Olympic Theater for one show and then walk around the corner to the Strand Theater for another or even down Court Street to the less desirable Victory Theater. Of course to get downtown in the first place, we'd hop on the city bus which would take us right to Public Square. On a really good day – most likely around the first of the month when Mom got her check from Dad, we'd even stop at the Crystal Restaurant on the Square for a western egg sandwich, topped off by their wonderful creamy, warm rice pudding. When ready to come home, we'd wait for the bus that had our street listed in its marquee and we'd take the return trip that deposited us in front of our house.

    With my tummy full of good food and my head filled with show tunes, my dreams that night would consist of being as talented and beautiful someday as Betty Grable or as good a dancer as Ginger Rogers.

    I can't help but wonder what the young children of today will remember as far as their movie-going years are concerned. Almost never do kids go to see a movie with real, living movie stars any more. Their choice of entertainment is relegated to animation figures, explosions, car chases, heroes and heroines that are drawn on some artist's canvas. And the entertainment from their television sets in their homes consists of Sponge Bob, Rugrats, Looney Toons and the like. Almost no heroes are real people. How can an animation figure be a role model?

    I remember renting a Jerry Lewis–Dean Martin movie for two of my grandchildren once, telling them how funny it was and how much I loved it as a youngster and hoping they would enjoy it. They reported back that they watched about half of it and decided it was not action-packed enough.

    I can't remember many movies being "action-packed." Watching Ginger Rogers and Fred Astaire waltz across the large screens, floating as if one person instead of a couple was not "action-packed."

It was a thing of beauty. Or we'd watch Esther Williams dive from a twenty-foot platform into a crystal clear pool, making it look effortless and surfacing with a gorgeous smile as only Esther could. And who could not enjoy watching Gene Kelly, Donald O'Connor and Debbie Reynolds splash their way through the classic "Singing in the Rain?" Will the children of today be whistling tunes from today's animated films when they are adults?

We kids were, however, able to get our fill of excitement by attending one of the weekly serial movies held in the basement of Sacred Heart Church. These were the days of one-hour action movies that ended up with the hero in terrible peril. He or she could actually be hanging on a cliff and be staring at a huge boulder ready to roll down to kill them. Thus, the term "cliff hangar" got its name from these movies. With Mom, we'd walk from our house to Sacred Heart Church and head down the side steps and into the darkened auditorium used for church fund raising events. We'd always spot kids that we went to school with or some of our neighbor friends.

To explain how the "pickle story" fits in here, I have to go back to a few hours before we attended one of the Sunday night shows at the church. A friend of mine, Nancy, lived a few doors away from me. She and I would often play "grocery store" or "restaurant" out back of her house. Her mother would supply us with a half-empty box of crackers or cookies, maybe some Kool-Aid or a miniature Hershey candy or two. These items would be displayed on a table as items for sale but would eventually be eaten by Nancy and me.

This particular day we ran out of food quickly so Nancy led me into her house and we opened the refrigerator trying to find more options for our "store." We saw a jar of dill pickles and there were at least five of them still left in the jar. That was good

51

enough for us so after adding that and an apple to our stash, we "storekeepers" went back to our jobs.

After washing down the crackers and cookies with the Kool-aid followed by the pickles, we split the apples in half. The pickle jar was now devoid of actual pickles and all it held was the pickle juice, a whole jar full of pickle juice, I might add. So I thought, "why not drink the juice?" I loved pickles so it seemed only natural to follow all our snacks down with a hefty cocktail of the juice. Down it went, little seeds on the bottom and all.

Our game was now ended and so I headed home to get ready to go with Mom and Margaret to the church basement to see how Flash Gordon was going to get out of his latest mess. This pickle juice event placed such a marker on my brain that I can even recall today exactly what dilemma Flash was left in the prior week. The bad guys had chased him and the beautiful Cynthia into a water tower. But they were locked inside and the water was turned on full force, causing them to have to keep climbing to the top of the tall tower. There was no escaping from above as it had a steel roof. The installment had ended there, leaving all us kids wide-eyed and frightened that they would have to end their movie career locked in that water torture chamber. All week long I tried to imagine in my wildest dreams how poor Flash and Cynthia would ever escape the death that was so imminent. I could not wait to get back to find out.

We entered the church basement, took our seats and shortly the room got darker, signifying that we wouldn't have to wait much longer. It was at that moment that my stomach started to pitch its first nauseating lurch. Then some hiccups started and all I could taste in my mouth was pickle juice. I really wasn't feeling well at all. But to let Mom know this would have meant an immediate end to my fun as she would have instantly taken my hand and led me to the bathroom in the rear of the basement. There were no speakers back in the bathroom and no way for me to keep my eye on the impending drama unfolding on the screen.

The movie started and I held my stomach in check just long enough to see Flash and his lovely girlfriend reach the top of the water tower. Suddenly, just when they were completely covered in water and on the verge of drowning, the top of the old tower burst open, spilling out its contents at the same exact moment that my stomach spilled its!

I pitched my body forward in my cheap fold-up chair with "SHC" stenciled on its back, and out came crackers and cookies, all colored red from all the strawberry Kool-aid. And in this horrible mess was pickle juice and more pickle juice. I was so sick that I think I literally was the same color as the former-red-now-turned-green mess flowing from under my shoes and down the aisle to the feet of all the unsuspecting little kids in the ten rows ahead of me. My only real regret of that night was that I had to miss that week's new cliff hangar and was forced to imagine what tragedy was bestowed on my beloved Flash without me there praying for him.

Sacred Heart Church was our home away from home. Back then, many significant events in our life took place in our parish. The usual Baptisms, First Holy Communions, and Confirmations were all held in the church but school events, movies, plays and holiday parties were held in its auditorium. Mom liked to take us to Bingo so that was an occasion to visit the basement which was as large as the enormous church over it. There were hundreds of banquet tables and chairs always available for whatever function was taking place. Mom belonged to the Altar Rosary Society and they held plays during the holidays. She would never act in them but would be sure to take us to watch the women of the club perform for the audience.

But the best part of that auditorium to me was for the party held at Christmas time. We'd get dressed up in our finest and sitting with some other kids I recognized, we'd be entertained by Christmas singers and dancers until finally Santa Claus himself would arrive He'd be accompanied by Mrs. Claus who would call our names and give us baskets of fruit and candy. And finally, after what seemed hours, Santa himself would call us up to the front of the room and we'd get a present of a doll or something as wonderful.

This took place for several years and I wondered why many of the kids in my class did not show up for this great event. It was after I went back to school after the holiday one January that I found out the reason. One of my classmates who never got these Christmas handouts informed me that these events with their free food and presents *were not for everyone, just poor kids like me.* I remember thinking how stupid that remark was. We were not poor. Were we? I didn't think so but I began to take stock of the kids who attended the free handout parties and those that did not. I came to the conclusion that she might have something there. The girls that wore the best dresses and had the newest shoes; the ones who had frequent Toni Perms and looked like Shirley Temple clones never attended. The ones who many brothers and sisters or missing or disabled fathers always attended. So that was it. We must be poor.

Fortunately, I never *felt* poor. Mom always made sure we had enough food in our stomachs and warm blankets in our beds. And later when she would take us to Sister Mathilde's to pick up whatever clothes we wanted, I thought everyone shopped there. But Sister Mathilde's Clothing Shop was similar to the Salvation Army except that we didn't have to pay anything at all. From time to time, Mom would volunteer to help Sister pack and distribute clothes to needy families, and so in exchange, we'd get to pick out a few skirts or blouses for school. So it worked out okay for a long time. But when I became a teenager, and because teenagers are notoriously self-centered, I did end up feeing deprived if not poor.

The church was also very familiar to us because of the many days and nights we attended services there. To Mom, attending Mass on Sundays was not enough. During Lent we would attend retreats, walking home in the dark after listening to a visiting priest give a powerful sermon, most often telling us we needed to do penance. Being good Catholic children, we did penance during the Lenten season and were encouraged to give up something we liked a lot. This sacrifice brought you closer to God during the six weeks that He was preparing for His ultimate sacrifice.

Most often our teachers would ask the children in my class to write some treat down on a piece of paper. This "treat" could be bubble gum (so desired during my youth) or candy or even movies. Then these pieces of paper were placed in a bowl on the teacher's desk and one at a time we would pick one out and take it back to our seat. When we read the scrawled word on the paper, we knew that this is what we would go without for Lent. I always wished it would read "movies" because during Lent my mother would not allow us to attend a movie anyway. So it would be no great hardship to get that slip. But if it read candy or bubble gum, I'd become pretty miserable. Interestingly, all the kids obeyed the rules of the "Sacrifice Game" and for the duration of Lent, we'd deprive ourselves of that goody.

We were strongly encouraged to save the pennies that we normally would have spent on the candy and gum and place it in the Pagan Baby Bowl and after Lent, the money acquired would be sent to the Missionaries in Third World Countries. The priests there, in turn, would provide food and clothing to needy families and in the process preach to them the word of God. What power I felt knowing I would keep a child from staying a "pagan"; a word I believed meant that the child didn't know how to pray, couldn't receive Holy Communion or end up in Heaven.

The Pagan Baby bowl became the receptacle of any extra penny I could talk Dad or Grandpa Ward out of. I'd like to think that there are hundreds of people in Heaven today because of my going without a Baby Ruth candy bar or a stick of delicious Double Bubble gum. And when some day I see them in Heaven (a little presumptuous of me – yes), will one of them yell out "Hey I was one of your Pagan Baby saves!" One can only hope. However, I will expect them to bring me some of those missed candy bars as reward!

Margaret and I figured out a way to obtain a few pennies at a very early age. Our brothers always purchased comic books such as Captain Marvel Junior, Superman and the like. The back cover of these books held interesting advertisements for ways to make some money in the 1940's, a time when a war was in full bloom. Selling a product called Cloverine Salve appealed to us so we'd save up the required two dollars and send it in to order our kit. This kit held about twenty tin cans of this "wonder salve", a remedy for almost any skin ailment.

When our kit finally arrived, we'd check out the contents of the kit and then head out to visit the surrounding neighborhood. Knocking on the doors of people we knew, we began our pitch trying to convince them that they *must* have Cloverine Salve in their bathroom cabinets.

If we were really lucky, we could walk away with a tidy profit of fifty cents or more each. We were pretty clever pre-adolescent entrepreneurs. But more than not, Mom ended up with the last five or so tins of the unsold product in her cabinet. I can still smell the rather putrid odor of Cloverine Salve today.

Katherine and Margaret - 1942

In front of our house on Stuart Street

Where "crepe paper plays" would be held a few years later

Margaret and

Katherine at

Olga and Bill's Wedding –

1947

(9 and 7 yrs. old)

Chapter 5

Older Brothers and Sisters Are Neat

Could an "only child" have this many memories?

    Having older brothers and sisters meant that we younger kids had a lot of people looking after our welfare. We looked up to these older siblings and have wonderful memories because of them.
    Our older sister Olga married Bill Sennett when we lived on Stuart Street. Olga was born fourteen years before me so I pretty much viewed her as a younger version of Mom. She spoiled Margaret and me and we were so excited to be a part of her impending wedding. I think Margaret was about nine and I was seven. Margaret wore a powder blue long dress to my white one. We wore flowers in our hair that Mom had meticulously brushed into long ringlets by rolling portions of our hair over her fingers. Looking back at Olga and Bill's wedding album, I'd say we were damned cute. The reception was held at Bill's parent's house on outer LeRay Street Road. This is where Olga lives today.
    I recall playing that day beneath the tree in front of the house with Bill's cousin, Shirley. Having all the food and soft drinks we wanted and just running around like lunatics with no adult telling us to "quit it" was rather fun.
    My brother Tom was the closest brother in age, being about five years older than me. He loved to sing country songs and yodel. Olga was also quite a yodeler and I always marveled at how she and Tom could get their throats to sound like they did. Tom seemed tall and lanky to me and he always had some time to spend with his two younger sisters. He was

funny and kind. He always had a joke or was ready to play some prank on Vern. Often he would clue me in on what was coming up. He was just a truly fun guy.

Tom worked on farms doing the typical outdoor chores. Once he came home with his face all scared and burned. A piece of machinery had blown up while he was operating it and he was lucky to have gotten off with only slight facial and hand burns. He was quiet a mess and Mom of course was frantic. However, she wasn't about to tell him to quit when the money he handed over to her weekly for room and board was so handy. Tom left school before graduating to get this job. It was pretty common then for boys to get as much schooling as they wanted, and then quit to start making some money.

Margaret and I were the only kids in our family to graduate. I only wish someone had encouraged me to go to college and fulfill my dream of being a nurse. I used to wait in the sidelines like a vulture for someone in the family to get sick. Because Vernon, Tom, Margaret and I were the only ones home when I caught the nursing bug, it had to be one of them that I hoped might catch some sort of illness. I'd love to do my nursing bit to help out and knew this was my calling.

On one of Dr. Ronson's visits to tend to someone sick at our house, he mentioned to Mom that it was obvious I might make a good nurse someday. He told Mom to contact him when I graduated high school and he would financially help me out with my dream. Unfortunately, Mom "doctor-shopped" as much as she "house-shopped". By the time I was in high school, Dr. Ronson was on her "hit list" of doctors and nowhere to be found. This could be for any reason. He charged too much, she heard of a better doctor, a cheaper one, a new one, a nicer one, etc. Pretty much the same justification that she used for all her house moves.

Later when my best friend Marilyn said to me in our sophomore year of school, "Let's be secretaries and then we'll move to New York City and get good jobs and marry rich guys," it sounded good to me. I was pretty fickle and left my lifelong desire for nursing on a whim. Besides, where was I going to get the money for nursing school anyway? So we took the business courses and became secretaries. Later, Marilyn moved away and left me stranded working as a secretary for a local manufacturing plant until I was so bored I thought I'd puke. Some dream!

I distinctly remember my brother Bill coming home from the war. I must have been less than six years old. Bill got out of a taxi in front of our Stuart Street house. Mom and Olga ran out to meet him and I remember peeking around the corner of the doorway, watching him as he got out, so handsome in his Navy uniform. He had been gone a while and I was kind of shy of him at first. He told Margaret and me that he had gifts for us. He had brought many souvenirs home from Japan and we couldn't wait to get our hands on them. I remember he handed something to Tom first, perhaps a knife or some such thing. Then just before our gifts, Margaret and I had some words, probably arguing over who would get the next gift. But in any event, it ended up with Bill telling us we would have to wait until later as a punishment for our bickering. He was Mom's son, that one.

Hours later he opened up his duffle bag and although I don't remember what Margaret got, I know I received a necklace of shells. There was a God! A necklace from Japan! I could not wait to go out and tell the neighbor kids the next day. The very next time we had our Stuart Street Backyard review, I wore a red crepe paper skirt, handkerchief top around my skinny bosom and those pink and white shells around my neck. The Andrew Sisters had

61

nothing on me that day. Boogie Woogie Bugle Girl indeed!

When I was in high school, we lived for a while next to Bill and his wife Alice. It was while there that Mom's first hands-on grandchildren were born. Michael Alan Taylor was the cutest little kid, long and skinny and so much fun to play with. A few years later a daughter Cheryl came along while we were at the same house, followed by David, Laura and John. I remember that well because it was so neat to be near my siblings when they had kids.

My brother Harvey and his wife Rosemary lived on the other side of Bill and Alice on East Lynde Street for a while and Donna Marie was their first-born child. Harvey was called "Red" for most of his life because of his russet colored hair, and Donna took on her father's trait. She was so cute and as she got a little older and I did too, Margaret and I were given the opportunity to baby-sit her for small periods of time. I loved reading her books and remember that she always sat so patiently on my lap and listened to me. I also remember being in her parents living room when I stupidly showed Donna how I could make music by tapping my teeth with a fork. My first unplanned visit to the dentist was the result of that escapade as I chipped a good size chunk from my front tooth. Funny how, because of the serious consequences of an event, it's so easy to recall much later on.

Harvey had a dog by the name of Bill. He was a beautiful red Irish setter. Today I can only wonder what our brother Bill thought of Harvey naming his animal after him. Perhaps Harvey acquired it from someone and it already bore that name. But we loved that dog so much. We were not allowed to have animals in our house because of Mom's serious allergy to them. If we went to a friend's house and played with their cat, her lungs knew it the minute we walked in the door. She would have to run to the cupboard and get her powder out, a strong smelling incense, and light it with a match. Then when the fumes rose up, she'd lean over the dish and breath in deeply, trying to get her breath back. We must have petted our friend's animals a lot, because I recall Mom doing that many times.

I had a cat by the name of Fluffy for a while. Well, I didn't actually *own* the cat but I made believe I did. It belonged to the people who lived next door to us when we lived on Grant Street. I pretended it was mine and would sneak food to it on a regular basis so it would like me. Mom used to be so mad that this darned cat was always coming to our front or back door. Didn't that cat know Mom was allergic to it, she'd wonder? I'd pretend I found it rather annoying too, but would slip out the back and call Fluffy back when Mom wasn't looking. I always tried to get all the cat hair off of my clothes but poor Mom would have another attack and she'd have to haul out the incense again. I began feeling pretty guilty and decided that Fluffy could no longer be my cat and so I ignored her until she felt it too. After all, why own a cat if you can't cuddle it and have it crawl all over you?

Big Sister Olga – So pretty (age 20)
Standing in front of a large snow bank at
our Grant Street home after the
huge December 1946 snowstorm.

Mom and Dad
In Front of our Pearl Street Road Farm House
1950 – Katherine (age 10) background

Chapter 6

John Frederick Taylor

September 15, 1924 - December 23, 1980

Brothers' returning home from the war was a way of life to us kids in the mid 40's. The Taylor boys joined the Army, the Navy and the Air Force and went off to either Germany, Italy or Korea. Our brother Jack served in the Army from 1942 to 1944 and became somewhat of a celebrity because he became a Prisoner of War. He was captured by the Germans and then a few days later made a daring escape. The following article is from our local newspaper, *The Watertown Daily Times* and was a featured article when Jack arrived home in 1944.

Pvt. John F. Taylor 19, of 228 Gale Street in Watertown, who served with the 7th Army in the invasion of Sicily and Italy, is back home today with a story of how he escaped from German imprisonment in a cave near Naples where he was held a prisoner for three days.
The youth, son of Mr. and Mrs. Ambrose W. Taylor, 670 Grant Street[7] is spending a 20-day convalescent leave with his parents. He has been in Army hospitals since his thrilling escape from the Germans on September 22.

---

[7] Interesting to note that we lived on Gale Street when Jack came home but yet our address was listed both as Gale Street in the first line and 670 Grant Street in the next. Obviously another move had taken place so quickly from one address to another that even the newspaper reporter had trouble figuring out where in the world we truly lived!

The solider, assigned to an infantry division in Gen. Patton's army, joined the Army on his 18th birthday and saw action at the front for more than two months. He was taken prisoner by the Germans early on the morning of September 19 while on patrol duty near an Italian village just below Naples.

Taylor and two companions were captured by six Germans armed with hand pistols and rifles as they were drinking water from a spring in the hills near Naples a few minutes after the Nazis had broken up the Allied patrol.

Marched to a desolate cave on the side of a hill overlooking an Italian village, the Watertown soldier and his buddies were there for three days. They made their break to freedom early on the fourth day when Taylor and his two companions overpowered three German guards, killing two of them.

Their break came when a Nazi soldier brought them food, he said. One of his buddies suddenly struck the German on the back of the neck, knocking the Nazi to the ground. They beat him into unconsciousness and then the three American soldiers surprised two guards at the entrance of the cave. Those Germans were overpowered and killed with their own bayonets, Pvt. Taylor relates. "Sure we were scared," he added. "After escaping from the cave, we ran for more than 30 minutes. We didn't

> know where we were going but we just kept running. Luckily we ran into one of our own patrols."
>
> Pvt. Taylor joined the service on September 15, 1942 and was sent overseas on June 2, 1943. He served first at Oran, North Africa and later at Bizerte.
>
> The local soldier was with the last wave in the invasion of Sicily, landing at Gela on July 10, 1943. From Gela, his infantry unit fought its way to Palermo and then to Messina where heavy German forces were encountered in the final battle of the island's conquest. After a period of rest, Taylor's infantry division was sent into Italy.

Jack returned home from the war in 1944, with a Purple Heart and Bronze Star in tow, to a great celebration by his happy family. As stated in the newspaper article, we were living on Gale Street at the time and although I don't remember how Jack got to our house that day, I certainly do remember him coming through the front door. I can still hear the cheers and yells of a family who were afraid they might not ever see their son and brother again.

Mom and Olga were crying and my brothers and Dad applied hard slaps of welcome on Jack's back. And I remember what happened next as clear as if it happened yesterday. It was my special moment with my adored older brother. I was watching all this take place from the corner in the living room. A typical reaction from an almost five year old trying to figure out just who this guy was. After all, he had been gone since I was not quite three years old.

Jack has his spiffy Army hat on and I thought he looked so regal and handsome. I stood there watching him and all the excitement that ensued around him. Then he came to me, swooped me up in his arms for a hug, calling me his "baby sister" and then deposited me in a standing position on the table. His last gesture was to remove that beautiful hat from his head and place it on mine, adjusting my hair as he did so. He and the party moved on into the living room.

I don't know how long I stood there wearing this heavy hat, but the next thing I knew Mom found me on the table smiling from ear to ear.

"How did you get up there?" she asked me.

I answered, "Jack put me up here."

That obviously was a funny thing to say because Mom went into the other room and repeated what I had said to everyone gathered there. I recall hearing laughter and wondered why it seemed so funny.

Looking back on that today, I believe because they were so filled with joy about the return of a son and brother who they feared they may never see again, that any thing or every word spoken seemed like a reason to celebrate. My standing on that table in my red and white dress with my droopy white socks and black patent leather shoes and an Army dress hat on my freshly curled hair is one of those Kodak moments that will forever be etched in my mind.

Chapter 7

Wash Day Blues

A detergent by any other name

    Jack was the brother that I didn't see much because once he was discharged from the Army, he married and settled in New Jersey with his wife Edna. He was the dapper brother, so neat in his freshly starched shirts and slacks. He almost always wore a hat on his head and he made me think that Dad must have been just like Jack when he was his age. Jack looked like Dad and acted like him in many ways. Jack also liked to drink like Dad. When they got a little tipsy, their stories could be volumes long.

    I remember Dad once visiting us kids when we lived on the corner of West Main Street and Curtis Streets. He had taken a "walk," most likely to a bar on Public Square, and came back in a very jovial mood. I could always tell when he was jovial because Mom was not! He began to tell Mom that she should wash her clothes using Super Suds like he did in his hotel room back in Deferiet where he was living. The more he described how he used that detergent to wash his white shirts, the madder Mom got and the more I felt ready to bust out laughing. The scene went something like this –

    Dad: "Mary, you should use Super Suds for the kid's laundry; it's the best."

    Mom: "I don't like Super Suds, Ambrose. I use Oxidol."

    Dad: "Well, I use it. I take a little Super Suds and make a paste with some water and then I place a little on my shirt collar and then I scrub and scrub and scrub. Then I take a little more paste - just love that Super Suds - and put a little more on the collar and scrub and scrub."

All the while he is telling her this, he is demonstrating by rubbing the imaginary soap between his two hands while balancing a cigar in his mouth. I think I remember this so well because it was so funny watching my father, a big man, always with the smell of cigars and a beer or two on him, telling my mother how to do the laundry, something she had been doing for nine kids for many years without his help, thank you very much!.

And Jack seemed so much like Dad to me. He was precise and as finicky as my father and very kind to Margaret and me when we were little. I remember being at his and his wife Edna's house at Easter time. We had Easter baskets filled with goodies waiting for us. We received more candy at their house than we did at home, a fact not lost on two sugar deprived kids during wartime.

The Easter baskets were actually colored pails that had a wax coating on them. You could scrape the wax off the outside and a drawing would be revealed under it. Just really cool. We'd eat the little yellow chicks and devour the red, black and white jellybeans until we thought we'd explode. Then we'd go home to open our own baskets and start all over again. Did I tell you my front tooth broke off real easy when I was little?

When Jack and Edna moved to New Jersey, we waited in anticipation for the phone calls from them, bringing us up to date on their lives. On December 31, 1946, the occasion of my 7th[th] birthday, I remember Mom receiving a phone call from them and I could tell she was getting some great news. Watching from the sidelines, I couldn't help but be caught up in the drama, although I had no clue as to what it was all about. Then Mom called me to the phone and said "Jack has something to tell you, Katherine." I took the phone and heard Jack tell me that for a birthday present, he and Edna gave me a baby nephew, Jackie Jr. I truly believed for many years that you could do that! If you wanted to, you could give this kind of a neat gift to someone on whatever day worked the best. So for a long time I thought Jackie Jr. was my birthday present.

Unfortunately, Jack and Edna later divorced and Edna moved away with Jackie Jr. For whatever reason, Edna and her son flew under the radar and my brother could not locate them. Jack, who had always liked a few 'toddies', began drinking in earnest around this time and his binges were mostly fueled by his longing for his missing child. Eventually, Jack also moved to Florida and remarried. He and his new wife Joan opened and operated a beer joint in Florida.

Working around alcohol for an alcoholic only quickens the decline into liver disease. This is what happened to Jack. He came home years later when he was very, very ill. He left Joan behind, apparently after a falling out between the two. I remember several of us going to the airport in Syracuse to pick him up and drive him home. I so clearly remember seeing Jack coming down the terminal with his luggage. He stomach was hugely distended with his alcoholism being in full blown mode. His face was pathetically thin and he looked so much older than he actually was. I turned and went into the bathroom for a minute so I could stop my crying before going back out. The change in him was pathetic. He was dying and we all knew it.

Jack lived for a few years more and even got a little better for a while. He rented an apartment on Emerson Street and almost every day when he was well enough, he'd saunter on down to Public Square and into one of the bars for a few drinks. He still looked dapper even then. He'd wear a straw hat and trench coat if it was cool out. I saw him many times walking along the east side of Public Square when I'd travel up Mill street to my home. There was no sense in offering him a ride as the Square was filled with watering holes and one of them would be his destination.

One day he walked all the way up Mill Street and ended up at our house on Cooper Street. I was alone and was so happy to see him. He was in no hurry that day so he and I sat on my front porch chit-chatting about the old days. He shared a lot of funny stories with me and then he came into the house to use my bathroom. He chose to use the one upstairs and when he started up and grabbed the railing, he found that a couple of the rails were loose. My husband Dick had been meaning to fix them but hadn't gotten around to it just yet. Jack took this opportunity to talk to me about safety, how Dick should get that fixed, how to do it and how he would do it if it were his house, blah, blah, blah, and all I could think was "Super Suds, Super Suds, this is how I would do it." Dad was back in my life.

One of Jack's deepest regrets was that his son was not a part of his life. He must have always wondered what kind of boy his son grew up to be and where he was living and what his occupation was. He told me in later years that he tried very hard for a long time to find Jackie Jr. but was unsuccessful. Ironically, when Jack and his second wife Joan were living in Florida, his son and his former wife Edna were in the same state, unbeknownst to Jack. Jack died from his alcoholism in 1983 without ever seeing Jackie Jr. again.

Chapter 8

"Jack, We Hardly Knew Ye!"

Title of the book by Dave Powers, on the life of JFK

About eleven year ago when Mom was still alive, I was talking to her about Jack and his son Jackie Jr. that none of us had ever seen. It was always obvious that her grandson's absence saddened her deeply.

When I went home I laid out a plan to see if I could find Jackie Jr. The Internet was not perfected in the manner it is today so I tried the old fashioned way of searching him out. I mainly used the telephone and the library. Olga filled me in a great deal on his mother Edna's place of birth and her maiden name and some of her family history. It seemed that Florida was the place to look and so that was mostly where I aimed my search.

I looked through old phone books at our public library trying to see if a family relative might still be in that state, but to no avail. Figuring that he was an adult now and would most likely be listed in the phone directory himself, I obtained a list of all John F. Taylor's in the southern Florida cities and over the course of the next month or so, called at least fifty of them with the lead question, "Is this the residence of John Frederick Taylor?" If I received an affirmative reply, I went on to ask if his parents were John and Edna. I always got either a "No" or a hang up. This was getting rather expensive.

After a while, I realized that a person's social security number was the key to finding them. But how do you obtain a person's social security number? And then if you have it, how do you use it in your search? I called our local social security office and told the person that answered that I was searching for my long-lost nephew and asked if his social security number would tell me where he lived? He said that it indeed could and that I should call the national social security office with any further questions. Armed with this information and excited about getting a little closer, I did call the national office and received disheartening news. You could not just call for and receive this information; it was private. Of course I already knew that but was hoping to get at least a little further. I let the matter drop after that but it was not very far from my mind.

About a month later on a visit with Mom in the nursing home, she brought the subject of Jackie Jr. up again, wondering if he was still alive and well. I went home with the search for him on the front burner of my mind once again. Mom's 95th birthday was coming up soon and we were planning on having the family all meet at the Ramada Inn for her birthday dinner. What a great gift I thought, if I at least had some information on him or better yet, him in person! I knew I was aiming high but I remember thinking that I would pray really hard and if God wanted this saintly woman to know a little bit about her long lost grandson before she herself left this world, then somehow I might be pointed in the right direction.

A few days later, I sat by the telephone, staring at it and wondering where to go next. It then dawned on me that perhaps I could yet reach a person at the national social security office who had a soft place in his or her heart. I called the number again, waited for about ten minutes to finally be connected to a live person and found that he was not only a live person but the one God directed me to. He had a kind sounding voice and knowing that this might be my last chance, I poured out the whole sob story of my poor aging mother, not having much longer on this earth, trying to find her dead son's child. It was all true and although I should have felt a little guilty about my tactics, I was on a mission to not get off that phone until I knew more about my nephew's whereabouts.

The man on the phone asked me Jack Jr.'s full name then some more questions about his parents, date of birth, and city and state of birth. I could tell that he was typing this information into his computer.

Then after a long silence, he almost whispered to me, "*I have his social security number in front of me.*"

I held my breath and asked him, "What do I do now?

He answered, "*I am totally not supposed to do this – it is against the law and I could lose my job, but if you want to, I'll tell you what city and state your nephew lives in.*"

I didn't breathe for a couple of seconds, sure he was teasing me. But then he said,

"*Your nephew lives in Aurora, Colorado.*"

I started to cry because I could not believe this day had finally come for Mom. I knew then why I never found Jackie in Florida. He obviously had moved out of that state when he became an adult. I wondered how long he had been living in Colorado, a state more than two time zones removed from us. I thanked the man on the phone profusely and I think he was crying too. He knew what a big favor he had granted me. Before he hung up, he said "*Good luck, honey.*"

The next day I started calling every John F. Taylor in Aurora Colorado. Surprisingly, there were more than a few. I asked each one if their middle names were Frederick and they all answered that it was not. On the very last call left to make, a woman answered and I simply asked her if "Jack" was there. She told me I had the wrong number. I hung up very disappointed and realized he might have an unlisted number and short of traveling to Aurora to check things out, I just probably wasn't going to find him.

That night as I lay in bed and went through in my mind, all the calls and the rejections I received, it dawned on me that on that one call where the female answered, I did not ask her if this was John Frederick Taylor Jr.'s home, only if "Jack" was there. What if he went by his real name of *John* and not by *Jack*? How stupid was I to not have pried further.

The very next morning I made the call again and an answering machine came on and a man's voice instructed callers to leave a number and he'd call back. I did leave a message stating that I was looking for John Frederick Taylor Jr. whose parents were John and Edna. I left my phone number and name and hoped for the best.

When I came home from work the next day, my answering machine was blinking with only one message. I hit the Play Button assuming it might be one of my kids calling. It was from *him*. He said,

"*This is John Taylor from Colorado. My parent's names were John and Edna. You left a message on my machine. If you want, you can call me when you get this, I should be home.*"

And that was it. I took a moment to think about what I was going to say and taking a deep breath and saying a short prayer, I called him.

When he answered I said, "Jack?"

He replied, "This is John; I don't go by Jack."

I told him who I was, all about his grandmother and why I had been trying to locate him. He told me that he had once tried to contact some Taylor's in Watertown but was unsuccessful. He seemed very happy to hear from me and was deeply saddened when I told him his father had passed away. There was a definite silence as he tried to digest this. He told me that he had always hoped his father was looking for him. I informed him that he had indeed tried to contact him on several occasions but always looking wrongly, in Florida.

We talked for quite a while and he described his job as a firefighter with the Aurora Fire Department. I told him about his grandmother's upcoming birthday and asked if would be possible for him to come see her. He was sad that he could not as he had reservations to fly to Australia shortly and would be there during Mom's birthday. This was a trip he had scheduled for a long time and involved other firefighters he worked with. He promised to send her a birthday card and photos of his children; Mom's great-grandchildren that she had never seen.

Jackie, now 'John', was surprised to learn that he was my personal birthday present many years earlier and he thought that was great. I then told him a few funny stories about his father, trying to conjure up some images that might make him know this missing figure in his life. There was a definite change in his voice and I could hear his sadness over the phone. It was very obvious that he was realizing all he missed by not having a father.

Jackie wanted to know how his father died. I thought for a moment – should I make up a story about his having cancer, a heart attack or some other ominous disease? But on the spur of the moment I made the decision to tell him the truth but in a toned down version. I told him that his father had developed a drinking problem that got worse as he got older. I went on to say that this caused him many serious health problems even though he quit drinking years before he died. His response to this was, "Boy, I understand that...I like to enjoy too many sometimes myself." *The apple doesn't fall far from the tree.*

At Mom's birthday party where I had dreamed of having Jackie pretend to be the waiter and he would come and surprise her and give her a piece of birthday cake, I had to settle for a card and photos of him as well as his lovely children and grandson. I asked for quiet from everyone and prepared Mom a bit for what was to come. I told her that there was someone who wanted to be with all of us today but could not but that he had written a beautiful birthday card for her. I then read it and when I got to the signature and said aloud "*Love, your grandson John*", she didn't get it.

I said "Mom, it's from Jackie Jr." She said "Who?" and I had to tell her a few more times. She was shocked to say the least. I sat down and showed her the photos of him and his children that she had never seen either. I told her of where he was living and explained why he could not be here. That was probably her most memorable birthday. I think she was always afraid he might be dead.

Later that week, I took my camcorder up to the Mercy Nursing Home where Mom was living. Olga went with me and we decided to record a little video and I would send it to Jackie Jr. Olga and I tried desperately to get Mom to just talk to the camera and tell Jackie what was in her heart. But for some reason, Mom thought it was like a letter and she'd start by saying "Dear Jackie..." After we convinced her that this was not a letter she was writing, she'd start again but found it too funny to talk to a camera. So she kept laughing, which in turn got Olga and I giggling too. I had to re-start that video over and over again until we could all get ourselves composed.

Finally calmed down, I said to her, "Okay Mom, I'll ask you a question and then I'll start recording your answer."

"Okay," she replied while wiping the tears from her eyes.

Then I started by asking her, "Now Mom, tell me what you thought of when you first heard that Jackie had been found?"

Instead of picking up the cue, this woman of the silent film era answered,

"Well, you know very well the answer to that Katherine, you were there!"

Olga and I again roared and told Mom that this wasn't what she was supposed to say; that I was taping her response and she should talk into the camera. So then I'd back up the tape and start again.

We were in such hysterics that even when I finally had film I could keep, you could hear Olga's snickers in the background and me trying to contain a snort of laughing. The final version shows Mom trying desperately to control herself from laughing out loud too. Mom could never have made it in a Judy Garland and Mickey Rooney movie!

I sent the video off to Jackie the following week and in a later phone call from him, he informed me that he was very happy to see all the relatives he never knew he had. And of course he was especially to see his father's mother. I felt my job was accomplished – finally!

Chapter 9

Mom's Last Residence

Warm At Last

Before Mom went to the nursing home where she lived until 1995, she lived in several of the senior citizen apartments in the Watertown area. Now it bears saying that even when Mom finally decided to stop renting apartments all over town and instead checked out the Watertown Subsidized Housing for Senior Citizens, she ended up living in all but two of them.

First, she moved to Skyline Apartments for seniors. She lasted there a few years but when she got sick one day, she decided that because her apartment was directly over the basement that held the building's oil heating system, she was allergic to the oil. So she made application to move from Skyline to another building for seniors across the street called Hilltop Towers. Before she could sign the paperwork, an opening occurred on the east side of town at a brand new complex and she could have it if she wanted it. Not being one to procrastinate when it came to making a move, she jumped at the chance. This one was brand new, shiny, freshly painted and ready for Mary Taylor to live within its walls. For how long, no one was sure.

Midtown Towers had just been built and because it was 'newer', 'nicer', 'warmer', 'cheaper' (familiar sounding pattern?); she had no problem telling the housing authorities the tale of her bad lungs and the contributions that Skyline made to them. So a call went out to all her children living in Watertown. She would need us on a Tuesday,

Wednesday or whatever day we were able to help her get those curtains back down out of the window.

Her furnishings were now dwindling a bit because each move necessitated, for whatever reason, that she pass off a few knick-knacks or odds and ends to the friends that she was now saying goodbye to. This made the moving a bit easier for those of us who would help her disassemble her bed, pack up (for the umpteenth time) her mis-matched dishes from the kitchen cupboards, and grab her dresses, blouses and dozens of bathrobes hanging from her closets. And let's not forget the dozen pairs of snuggies, still her favorite garment for keeping warm in the winter.

Once the move was made and her furnishings now arranged in her new living room, kitchen and bedroom, Mom would go about hanging the curtains in the new house to make it seem like home. The art of curtain-hanging was taken very seriously by my mother. A house was not a home unless the bright and perky curtains were hanging in each room. It was if that made these new surroundings comforting and familiar to her.

Next it would be the task of my sisters and me to help her arrange furniture and various other items in the apartment. We'd help her decide where each piece of furniture, end tables and lamps should go. We'd line her kitchen shelves with colorful shelf paper and place her cups and dishes convenient for her to take down. This of course would be all undone in about ten days. The next time you visited and wanted a cup of coffee, your hand would reach for the cup and as you drew it to you, you would see that it was laden down with sugar from the nearby sugar bowl or salt from the turned over salt shaker. Mom may have been clean and ready to chase down any germs in her house, but neat she was not.

Mom lasted at Midtown Towers until she heard that there was new senior housing going up at

Curtis Apartments on West Main Street. This building was located at the site of the old Immaculate Heart Academy, which housed a chapel. She figured that to live in that building would be like living *in* the chapel. So off she went. Interestingly, her apartment *was* located approximately where the chapel was; a fact not lost on my mother.

During the times that Mom lived in these apartments, her children were marrying and having their own children. On Sundays, it was practically mandatory that we all end up at Mom's apartment for coffee, donuts or cookies after church. The kids played with one another and stuffed sugar in their mouths while my brothers and sisters and I brought each other up to date on our lives. These visits were truly the highlight of Mom's week. As Mom's grandchildren got older and had a variety of other things to do after church, my brothers and sisters and I would continue this ritual until the get-togethers eventually took place in the nursing home.

The need for a move to the nursing home was primarily because of my mother's failing eyesight. She was diagnosed with macular degeneration when she was in her eighties. Her vision became increasingly worse and was of much concern to all of us. This very cruel eye disease strikes more people now than ever before or perhaps with early detection; it is just being diagnosed easier. The American Foundation for the Blind summarizes on their website www.afb.org, the condition thusly:

> "Age-related macular degeneration (ARMD) is the leading cause of vision loss among older Americans. The macula is the small area in the center of the retina that makes sharp detail vision possible from the center part of the eye. Macular degeneration results in blurred or distorted central vision or a central

blind spot called a scotoma. When central vision is impaired, older people have difficulty recognizing faces and colors, driving a car, reading print, or doing close handwork, such as sewing or other handcrafts.

Age-related macular degeneration results in a gradual distortion and sometimes complete loss of central vision. Although age-related macular degeneration has the effect of creating a "blind spot" in the center of the field of view, vision outside the central field is not affected. Macular degeneration alone does not result in total blindness."

As her vision worsened and other physical ailments related to old age developed, it was apparent that Mom would need some assistance. She was now 93 years of age, still pretty spry and definitely had all her mental faculties. But living alone around hot stoves, tea kettles and other scary potential accidents-in-waiting forced us and her to re-think her living arrangements.

She had many friends who were in the local Catholic nursing home called Mercy Nursing. She loved that hospital and she and other friends would often visit the occupants there and afterwards attend the noon Mass in the chapel. Knowing that she could be practically living in a church gave her no qualms at being interviewed by the authorities to determine her own need. The public health nurse that came and examined Mom and her current living arrangements decided that her eyesight put her at high risk for living alone and recommended that she be placed on the top of the list of applicants.

An opening occurred shortly afterwards and Mom happily agreed to this new move. Once again we helped her clear out her apartment but this time she gave away almost all of her belongings to friends in the building and to family members. We held a rummage sale, clearing out many items that would not be needed any longer. She gladly participated in this with us, enjoying the bartering that went on with those who stopped by to check out her belongings.

    So off to the nursing home she went. The transition went pretty well. She was excited at first (after all this was a *move*), but not to be out of character, after her first week there, she wanted to move down the hall to another room, namely room 407. Her current room was a bit drafty and not as large as this other one she had her eye on. Of course the fact that room 407 was already occupied by another woman did not deter Mom. She had me inform the supervisor that at the first opportunity (this had to mean the demise of the current occupant) my mother would be very interested in acquiring that lovely and warmer room.

    Mom took daily walks around the large halls and soon became a very beloved resident. The nurses loved her and because she loved to visit the sick and defenseless, Mom spent a good deal of her day chatting with them. This also provided her with a perfect opportunity to visit the occupant of 407 and admire in closer detail, the niceties of this room. She became pretty good friends with this woman also named Mary, but unfortunately Mary was very deaf and Mom being a 'low talker', it was not easy for them to converse.

    A few months later, Mom told me that Mary had died. Mom was very upset as she had become very fond of her. She was so upset that she didn't even mention the fact that the room was now available. I was with Mom when the supervisor came into her room and asked her if she still wanted to move to 407 as it was now available. Mom was so eager that within the hour she was settled nicely in

Mary's room, praying I'm sure, for the repose of her soul and thanking her for her lovely room.

Before moving to the nursing home, Mom was surrounded by other residents of Midtown Towers on each side of her and so we always felt she was in pretty good hands and didn't need daily visits. Consequently, my brothers and sisters and I would visit about once or twice a week. But when she was at Mercy Nursing, my family felt that she was now alone so we scheduled our visits so that one of us would visit her daily. She had more visitors than anyone on the floor ever had. Also she loved to leave the nursing home to go to lunch or dinner or to visit her friends or a family member. This necessitated us signing her *out* in a book when we took her out and signing her *in* when we retuned her. Most residents left the home about once a month if lucky, but Mom came and went so much, many residents probably thought she was on staff!

After her first year there, she complained to Olga and me one day that she didn't get out very much. The two of us raised our eyes in disbelief over this statement and then took a walk to the nurse's station and asked to check the sign-out book. In the previous year, she had been taken out by one family member or another over 100 times! We told her this and she shook her head and "tsk – tsk'd" this as if it were all part of a plot. She could be so darn funny!

Chapter 10

Stuart Street Meltdown

"I'm feeling a little gassy tonight"

As I stated at the beginning of this book, my first memory of any significance was when I was eight years old. The only reason I would remember this particular event is because it almost ended in my death.

We were living on Stuart Street at the time and Mom was having trouble with our coal furnace. She had words with our landlord about getting it fixed and he had promised to take care of it. I'm not sure how long we had lived in this house; the house of the crepe paper skirts, mud-pies and hollyhock flower-dolls, but I do know it was our second move there. We had lived there when I was about 2 or 3 years old and for some reason we returned to occupy its walls once again. One stopped asking "why?"

Having trouble with a furnace, broken locks on doors, missing screen windows and so on was the norm with us. I know that because those were some of the reasons that bothered Mom so much, that she'd rush to scour the apartment rental section of the newspaper. But for a furnace to not work properly was of real concern during the days when a coal furnace was the usual form of home heating.

Coal furnaces are all but extinct now. In the late 1960's and early 70's, a Federal Law was passed to help clean up the environment. The Clean Air Act and Clean Water Act outlawed coal as a main heat source because of the organic sulfur; a substance that is chemically bound to coal. This contributed greatly to acid rain and the greenhouse effect and therefore furnaces were upgraded to oil, gas or anything but coal. But in the late 40's, houses all around the big cities, small cities and even in Watertown, New York, were heated almost exclusively by coal. And so was our house located on Stuart Street. Mom was a very light sleeper and because this I owe her my life.

One winter night, our faulty furnace leaked dangerous carbon monoxide because of a serious malfunction. Obviously the landlord knew of this because he had told Mom that he would be getting back soon to fix the furnace as it had a "problem." Carbon monoxide is an odorless and highly poisonous gas which is deadly when breathed for any length of time. But thank God Mom's hearing was sharp. She and I were the only ones to sleep on the ground level in our house. The rest of my siblings slept in upstairs bedrooms and were not aware of the events unfolding downstairs.

As Mom related it, she was in her bedroom, which was located right next to mine. The unfortunate part for me was that my bedroom was situated right over this toxic spewing furnace and I was receiving its gases, full force. Mom woke to the sound of my moaning. At first she thought I was having a nightmare but then became alarmed and came into my room to check on me. She tried to wake me up but was unsuccessful. At the same time, she realized she had a bad headache and felt dizzy. Fearing the worse, she called up to Olga who came down the stairs and informed Mom that something was very wrong.

My recollection of some of that night is as vivid today as it was back then. I woke up in Olga's arms, wrapped in a quilt. She held me next to an open back door off the kitchen. It was very cold and snowy as it was December, and the crisp, frigid air brought me out of the unconscious state I had just been in. Then I remember no more until I awoke on the couch, crying and wet in my urine-soaked pajamas and seeing Mom, Olga, and Tom. Other members of my family were most likely there also but I only remember them. Other than family members, I definitely remember men in uniform, namely several firefighters and eventually Dr. Ronson who Mom must have phoned and who paid a house call. (This was before her putting him on her "hit list" of physicians.) After getting over the shock of seeing all these people staring at me, I allowed the doctor to examine me. He decided to have me taken to the hospital where he could watch me overnight.

Waking up the next morning in the children's ward of Mercy Hospital was very scary. I watched as a boy about my age was having bandages removed from his badly burned stomach. His screams of pain were enough for me to beg Mom to let me come home that day. But the doctor felt I should stay a day longer so I had an opportunity to meet Georgie, the little boy who had been so disfigured in a fire.

I learned that he had been severely burned when he was only six months old. Apparently he was in his highchair and was left next to a stove. He threw something into the fire and the results were tragic. He was hospitalized many times over the years and eventually had one leg amputated. I have seen him in various situations many times since then, practically running with his one crutch. His tragedy didn't seem to slow him down at all. There is no reason for him to remember me occupying a bed near him in the pediatric ward so many years ago, but I will never forget him

As I said, I was lucky that Mom had her bedroom close enough to mine to hear me. It seems her bedroom was always close to mine and sometimes her room was my room too! As I got older and my siblings moved out to marry or leave the area, the houses we lived in had fewer bedrooms. Consequently, I shared many bedrooms with Mom. If I wasn't sleeping *in* her bed, I was in a smaller one right next to hers. Mom always wore a big corset under her clothes, not only to keep 'it all in', but because she had a bad back from carrying ten children. Every night she took this seemingly ten pound corset off her body and would throw it on my bed. I hated that thing being thrown on me and I think the more I protested, the more she tossed it my way. It was her way of telling me she was still in charge. I could not wait until I moved out and had a room where no corset-tossing would ever take place again. I'm happy to report that my husband never did that to me.

But eventually after my near-death experience I did come home from the hospital and was not quite the same for many years. I was diagnosed with a large heart and it took about five years for this malady to leave me. But what stayed with me embarrassingly way too long was the urgent need I had to go to the bathroom *at once!* Apparently my kidneys were affected in some way by the toxic fumes and it had consequences that would haunt me at the worst possible times and in the worst places for years to come.

It seems like whenever we were in church (which was often if you were Mary Taylor's child), the urge to go *now* would strike me without notice. I think it became a common sight to those in attendance, to watch me leave my seat, traipse up the side aisle and go behind the altar where I would eventually find the bathroom.

Bathrooms were not located with the congregation in mind back in the 40's and 50's. They were primarily used by the priests and altar boys and obviously were not expected to be used by the churchgoers. I used to think that people in their pews were thinking "Well, there goes that little girl again. My, can't she ever get through Mass without having to go to the bathroom?" The answer to that, if they had asked *me* would be "No!"

Chapter 11

Things I'd Rather Forget

It shouldn't hurt to be a kid

     Statistics show that in the period from 1986 to 1993, one fourth of all girls before the age of sixteen have been molested. Sadly, less than 6% of them were ever reported to an authority figure. I don't know what the statistics were in the early 1950's but it happened to me and I certainly never wanted to tell a living soul. That's the real tragedy of this heinous crime.

     I have never revealed exactly what happened to me during my pre-adolescent years nor will I use this venue to do so now. I have hinted to a couple of members in my family about *some* of the incidents, but choose to keep the worst ones hidden deep somewhere in the recesses of my soul. I have since learned that in coming to grips of what a child takes with them in their journey into adulthood, along with the good, the sad, and the funny, there is also the ugly. My molester was male, known to our family but certainly never suspected of being the type to mishandle one of the young and vulnerable Taylor girls. However, it did happen over a period of a two years and I felt I had no control over the situation. I often wondered what would happen to him if Mom or my older brothers ever found out. But sadly, I was not strong enough to take that chance by confiding in anyone.

     I remember later in my teenage years wanting to ask my schoolmates, any one of them, if this ever happened to them. But they were so attractive and cool and seemed so all-together, that I was sure I was the only one in the whole school who had ever had to keep such a deep, dark secret. Perhaps because I was very gawky, scrawny and clumsy at age ten and eleven, that this made me a prime target. In any event, I endured it, stuffed it away somewhere in my memory bank and was so happy when, for whatever reason, it all stopped. It does seem amazing that after something like this happens to you; you can actually go on with the rest of your life and not think about it on a daily basis.

Today so many television shows deal with the subject of molestation. It is not taboo to talk about and there are so many tips on how to receive help if you are young and the object of unwanted and uncomfortable attention by an adult.

I was watching one of these very shows when I was in my thirties. It was a popular talk show and the host had several women who had been abused as youngsters as her guests. While listening to their conversations of how they had come face to face with what had happened to them, my memories of what took place so many years ago came flooding back to me like a torrential downpour. I didn't react in that moment; not that day or the next. But about two weeks later while alone in the house watching a made for TV movie where the heroine had also been molested as a child, something triggered the emotions and pain that had been so long buried. I cried so hard for the little girl in me that had endured such frightening experiences and I was so sad that I had not been able to tell someone to help me make it stop.

From that day on, I recognized it and realized that I was a survivor and it also explained many things to me; things that made me react in certain ways or even dream certain dreams. I was able to understand a lot, forgive a lot and become more interested in the subject and its impact on society today. How many thousands and thousands of adults today have been victimized as children and how different are they in certain ways because of that victimization?

As a sad footnote to this, when I was thirteen and finally beginning to feel safe, I had another experience that scared me again. After visiting a girlfriend's house one day, I decided to take a shortcut home. As I left my friends house, I realized that if I walked the railroad tracks behind the stores on Factory Street, I could save some time on my way up Mill Street to my final destination, one of our many houses on the city's north side.

A few minutes into my journey, I looked ahead and saw a man of about thirty years of age standing on the other side of the tracks. As I proceeded, he stepped over the rails so that my path would now take me directly in front of him. Keeping my head down, I continued on my way hoping that in broad daylight, this guy would prove to be no threat. But soon he was in front of me and much to my surprise and horror; I noticed that his pants (both of them) were now down around his knees! I immediately took off on a dead run past him, through an alleyway to get to the Factory Street sidewalk. I ran like a track star the rest of the way home. Lucky for me, it would have taken him a minute or two to get his pants back up so I knew I could outrun him.

When I finally entered the safety of my house and into our living room, Mom was there, listening to Arthur Godfrey and ironing some of the clothes in the never-empty laundry basket.

"How come your face is so red? Have you been running?"

"Yeh, I wanted to get home and listen to my new record."

That was a believable fib as I was always trying to save up another 49 cents so I could buy the latest 45 RPM record, hurry home and play it for hours.

There was no way I would have told her what had just occurred and I'm sad that I felt that I could never share my bad experiences with her.

Chapter 12

I Get To Be an *'Only Child'*

"My name's Janice – what's yours?"

When I was about ten years old we moved to Summer Street, located on the west side of town. Once again I was the new kid on the block and didn't know any of the kids I saw playing in the neighborhood. It was winter time and when I discovered that the Ninth Ward Playground was located only two blocks from our house, I decided to go and check it out.

I found that it had a huge ice skating rink and on top of that, close by was a steep hill where kids could go tobogganing, if of course, one had a toboggan. We Taylor kids did have a couple of old sleds that made the move with us to each new home, so I ran back home, got the best one out and lugged it back to the playground.

When I returned, the hill was now abound with kids, all careening down the hill at topnotch speeds and coming close to crashing into the big old elm tree at the bottom. The tree was surrounded by a small stream that was only half frozen over and so this made the ride all the more exciting. Two or three kids had obviously ended up in the water as their snowsuits bore ice-trimmed cuffs and collars.

A couple of kids came near me with their sleds, snot running from their red flushed faces to gave me the once over. No one seemed all that friendly so I proceeded to drag my sled up the hill, enjoy the ride down, trying desperately to avoid that tree and the potential for a broken bone. Finally, too cold to stay any longer, I dragged my sled behind me all the way back home, wishing so badly that I had someone to enjoy this with. My chance came about a week later when I decided to go back and check out the skating rink.

I didn't have any skates that fit me but I knew that my brother Tom did, so I went to the large hall closet and found his beat-up old pair, more than gently worn and dark black in color. Not caring what they looked like but worried about the size, I grabbed a pair of heavy socks from Tom's dresser drawer, slung the skates over my shoulder and headed for my Hans Brinker moment, informing Mom that I'd be back in about an hour or so.

It was beginning to get a bit dark out at this point and the temperature was rapidly dipping. Raising my muffler up over my nose, I hurried as fast as I could, longing for the warmth of the shed where I could put my skates on.

Ice skating sheds usually held a huge pot bellied stove and the rink attendant would keep it plied with wood, allowing the frozen skaters a moment or two to thaw out. Entering the shack, I found that this one was no different and so I settled down onto one of the benches. Looking around once again for a smile from someone, but not receiving any, I attempted to lace up the clumsy skates. I soon did receive some attention from a couple of the girls nearby but not the kind of attention I was looking for.

"Those are ugly boy's skates", said the little priss-ass sitting across from me. Ignoring her and her laughing friends, I finished lacing the skates and headed for the door to try out the ice.

It was then that I discovered that these skates were approximately four or five sizes larger than my feet. And the one pair of woolen socks I wore did little or nothing to change that fact.

Everyone was zooming past me at top notch speeds. My feet were wobbly and my skinny ankles proved no match for the huge skates that perfectly fit my older brother. I had only skated a few times before in my whole life but thinking that perhaps the faster I skated, the more upright I would remain, I lowered my head, wound up my arms as if ready to take flight and drove forward in a frenzy.

You may have seen the Disney movie, *Bambi*. Bambi too had a horrific time on the ice and as he attempted to conquer it, his legs went askew and he plopped down, face first onto the ice, making an embarrassing spectacle of himself. Bambi had nothing on me.

The faster I plowed ahead, the less control I had. I could see the huge snow bank ahead of me and before I could attempt to veer from its' path, it was upon me, or more aptly, I was upon it!

My head drove into the soft snow bank and the only part of me that protruded was the lower half of my body from my waist down. It took a minute for me to pry myself from the snow bank's grip. My head was now wrapped in a white turban of snow and when my vision cleared, I discovered that I was looking directly into the face of one of the prettiest girls I had ever seen.

Looking down at me, this girl who appeared to be about my age smiled and said "Boy, you don't skate very good, do you?" Clearing the last remnants of snow from my eyelashes, I stood up on trembling legs and took a good look at her. Wearing a white parka jacket with pink fur around her pretty face, matching pink angora mittens and muffler around her neck, pure white and perfectly sized white skates on her feet, she was everything I was not.

My skating costume consisted of my sister's hand-me-down red snow pants, a brown jacket that matched nothing, a way too large green muffler around my skinny neck, one blue mitten and one brown mitten and an old ski hat on my head belonging to one of my older brothers. And then of course there were the skates! Clothes and fashion had never meant a thing to me until that moment.

Who knew you could look this pretty and enjoy a sport?

"My name's Janice – what's yours?" she asked. I told her that my name was Katherine and that I knew I wasn't skating very well today because I had on my big brother's skates. I went on to explain to her – actually lie to her - that normally I was an expert skater.

At this point, she pointed across the street to a beautiful large house on the corner and told me that this is where she lived. She asked me if I wanted to come over to have some hot cocoa and warm up a bit before we continued skating.

Later while sitting at her kitchen, warm mugs in hand, I inquired as to where her older brothers and sister were. The house was painfully silent with only her mother in the other room reading the newspaper. Janice informed me that she was an only child. *An only child?*, I mused. How amazing that I had never ever met anyone who was an only child! She was equally amazed to find out that I was the youngest of nine children and immediately ran to the living room to impart that startling bit of news to her mother.

In the years to come after that accidental meeting, Janice and I became the best of friends. Her family included me in every detail of their lives and I loved going to Janice's home and being treated as if I were her sister. How great was this? Plus - they had an automobile!

Her parents took us for rides into the country and we'd watch the cows grazing in the fields of the many farms that occupied Jefferson County. We would stop for ice cream cones and sing silly songs on the way home. Then they would drop me off to my house where quickly I reverted back to being the youngest of nine children.

But by far, the best part of being her friend was being her friend in the summer. Janice's grandparents lived on a farm near Pillar Point. We would beg her parents to take us to the farm where we would play in huge fields, chasing chickens, exploring large barns and trying to catch the wild kittens which roamed its two levels.

My very first experiment with smoking happened in the summer of 1952 while at the farm. Janice and I did not have access to real cigarettes but somehow she had heard that you could actually smoke the stalk of the corn growing in her grandparent's field. We discussed this at length for a while and then a week or so later, armed with the actual "how to" of this adventurous undertaking, we attempted to smoke our first corn stalk. If this were a television show, there would be a disclaimer at the bottom warning people "*Do not attempt this yourself.*"

Lighting and actually inhaling the stalk of corn on the cob was not the high we were expecting. The burning sensation all the way down our lungs was nothing we wanted to repeat. It was if we had actually inhaled the flames. After coughing and gagging for a long time and finally getting back our breath, we looked at each other, laughed hysterically and knew instinctively that this was something that would never be repeated. From that day on, the closest we got to farmer's corn again was to help her grandparents shuck it before dinner. Of course each time we did, we gave each other a sheepish glance and grin, sharing our little secret. I'm not sure how many years it took before our seared lungs healed, if ever.

Later that fall, I was invited to go with my "other family" to New York City for a week to visit some of their relatives. It was in the 1950's and Times Square was alive with colorful stores, theaters and vendors but yet we were safe and felt no fear walking the streets, just the two of us alone. Janice's parents stayed in the hotel and allowed us to walk two blocks to a bowling alley. I can still recall the freedom we two twelve year olds felt while gawking at the huge billboards and marveling at the Marlboro Man blowing smoke downward at those of us walking through the teeming city streets.

Many years later as an adult, I returned to walk those same streets again. Much had changed. It seemed very seedy and dirty, and strangely I didn't feel as safe as I had thirty years earlier as a child with my best friend by my side.

About this time in our lives, Janice informed her parents that she would like to take tap dancing lessons. I talked Mom into letting me take lessons too. Even though this was most likely considered a frivolous expense to a woman like Mom, she agreed. I wasn't too surprised. After all, Mom was the one who had the original wanderlust for Broadway; had instilled it in us kids by dragging us from movie theater to movie theater and most likely dreamt that one of her daughters could actually make it on 42nd Street one day.

So every Saturday morning, off Janice and I would go on a city bus to the dance studio located on Public Square. When not actually in the studio taking tap dancing lessons, first from Mr. Van, an extremely tall man who made me think of Fred Astaire, Janice and I tapped ourselves silly. Any solid floor was our dance studio. Janice's kitchen with its vinyl floor was great for producing the loudest taps. Banging out the steps to Sammy Davis Jr.'s "Mr. Bo Jangles", we were in seventh heaven.

On warm summer days when not at the family farm, Janice and I held Kool-Aid sales in her front yard and played jacks and basketball in her huge driveway. And the year her family hosted a Fresh Air child from New York City, the two of us learned the most amazing jump rope moves from Julia, the first black girl either of us had ever known. Julia was from the Bronx and seemed so worldly to Janice and me, and we appeared like county bumpkins to her.

We learned a lot from her but mostly we learned that kids are the same no matter your ethnicity or place of birth. Julia laughed as hard as us at the same goofy jokes, knew how to make soda spurt out her nose like we did and taught us the lyrics to all the songs we heard on the radio. She, in our small-town eyes, was so wise.

Janice's parents loved to spend their summers in cottages in Adams Cove, a wonderful summer spot for vacationers wanting to live by the water. Adams Cove sported a great hang-out called Stumble Inn. The juke box that sat alongside the dance floor was surrounded by about twelve wooden booths, all crammed with other teenage summer campers.

Listening to songs by Teresa Brewer and Brenda Lee while sipping cherry cokes, we'd try to catch the attention of the good looking boys who scanned the room, ready to ask one of us to jitterbug. Even if we didn't get asked, we'd sit in those booths until Janice's father would come to the Inn's door and motion that it was time to call it a night.

When not at the farm or vacationing at the cottage, our boredom was relieved by shopping in all the wonderful stores in downtown Watertown. I say *shopping* but actually we'd just spend time looking at all the great items that we planned to buy once we graduated and had jobs. We'd go into Empsall's Department Store, one of the city's premier stores for clothing, shoes, handbags, hats, jewelry and other delights. We'd ride the elevator up to the second floor and try on all the lady's hats. We'd each go to a different display table and try to find the funniest one. Plopping it on our head, we'd turn to look at each other and die laughing until the saleswoman would scold us and ask us to leave. Running across the street to Barbara's Hat Shop, we'd act a bit more sedate and actually pretend we wanted to purchase one of these elegant feather-bearing beauties.

Now bored with the hat game, we'd wander on down Court Street a bit and head for the Globe Store, an equally interesting place to have fun. Spraying on all the perfumes and colognes in the cosmetic section would leave us smelling like a couple of French whores. There too, we'd eventually be asked to move on.

I had so much fun with Janice. Roller skating at the Fairground's to the organ music of the very talented Jack Briceland, attending birthday parties and "spin-the-bottle" parties where I experienced my first real kiss, crawling under the fence to sneak into the Jefferson County Fair, only to be caught and sent back out and forced to pay the required 50 cent entrance fee; we crammed a lot of memories into the three years we were "best friends".

Summer fun ended, fall and winter brought new adventures and the years flew by. Soon we were both in high school where Janice was a freshman to my being a sophomore. And as happens too often, she took up new friends in her circle as did I. But I will always remember the wonderful times I spent with her and the opportunity to feel spoiled as only an "only child" can.

Chapter 13

Losing a Parent

Ambrose W. Taylor
January 14, 1892 – September 23, 1952

    In 1952 when I was an 8th grade student at Holy Family School, Dad suddenly appeared in our life again. He had been very ill with lung cancer and was still living alone in Deferiet, NY where he had lived since separating from Mom a good many years earlier. Mom, Tom, Margaret and I were living at East Hills Apartments. Without telling us why, Mom announced that Dad would be coming back home and would be staying there. We later found out that she had been told he had just six months to live so she felt obligated to take care of this man who was still officially her husband.

    What I remember most about my father being with us, was his sitting by the radio listening to Arthur Godfrey and pretty much making fun of the man. Mom liked the show and it was her house so the radio was tuned to the Godfrey Show on a daily basis. At almost every statement Arthur made, Dad one-upped him with a "Humfff" and some sort of derogatory comment. Obviously, Ambrose and Arthur would never have been friends if they had met.

    One night in September of that year when I was twelve years old, I was awakened by the sound of footsteps and frantic running back and forth in the upstairs bedrooms. I peeked out my room to see Dad running back and forth in the hallway and finally to the open hallway window where he thrust his head out into the cool night, trying to grab some much needed air into his dying lungs. I next remember being downstairs and seeing Olga. Tom had been working the night shift for a taxi company and he was called home and so he finally appeared too. I walked back up the stairs and looked in the bedroom to find Mom standing over Dad who was in a kneeling position by his nightstand. Mom was sprinkling holy water on him and placing the crucifix on his head, all the while praying loudly for her dying husband.

I ended up in the bathroom where I was suddenly ill. I waited in this room, the only place that seemed to be safe, until the commotion ceased outside its walls. Finally I gathered the nerve to walk out and passed Dad's room without turning to look. He was gone; it was evident by the look on everyone's face. I remember not feeling much of anything but fear. I did not really know this man. He was the person who visited us monthly from a village not far away. He brought us chocolate candies and it seemed like the best candies always arrived during the Lenten season. I always gave up candy for Lent and once Lent was over, so were the candies, eaten by those in the family who had given up a different sacrifice for forty days.

I envied my older brothers and Olga who knew Dad so much better than Margaret and I did. They had a special bond with Dad and could, and still do tell funny stories about their relationships with this man who was almost 50 years old when I was born.

The wake was held at the Hart funeral Home. Mom planned to have all of us kids attend of course, but when she told me that my teacher was bringing my classmates that evening, I knew could not go. I wouldn't know what to say to them and the thought of standing in line in front of my father's casket greeting them was absolutely petrifying for me to think about. So I claimed illness and stayed home but the next day I did go and thankfully none of my friends were there.

Dad's wake and funeral were the first I had ever attended and it still leaves a searing memory in my brain of sadness, family, hugs, laughter and all the mixtures that accompany the compilation of mourners in one room designated to say goodbye to someone so many people loved, admired or in my case, really didn't know well at all.

Olga, Bill, Minnie and Mike (Bill's parents), Dad and Mom Summer Street, Circa 1950

Buddies – Tom and Vern – Circa 1950

Vern looks just like Dad here! Vern sent this photo to Tom and wrote on the back: "Remember this? I thought ya might like to see it again. *Never and Always* by Lefty Frezel is on the radio. Vern"

The Famous Taylor Brothers!
Good Old Stock Car Days
L to R - Harvey, Jack, Bill and Jim
Vern (Fence Buster) inside his stock car.

Chapter 14

Love is a Many Splendored Thing

So many perfect songs for sappy teenagers in love!

     Olga had been the sister that we younger kids had so depended on and then suddenly she was gone. When she married and moved out of the Stuart Street house we all shared, that was traumatic enough. But to make matters worse, she and her husband Bill moved to the complete opposite end of the world. Or that's how it felt to me. Who knew how far Florida was anyway? I was 12 years old and never been further then Brownville and now Olga and Bill were living in Pensacola, Florida where Bill ended up as part of his job for the paper mill. I missed her terribly and my letters to her demonstrated that.
     Olga had kept every single letter that anyone in our family wrote to her during their time in Florida. We were obviously quite the letter writers and thank God she saved every one of them.[8] They were from Mom and Dad and each one of my brothers and Margaret and me. In 1996, Olga showed me the letters from us to her. I was fascinated by them and the love that we all felt for her was echoed in each of our writings. I saw my pre-teen handwriting and read the flowery prose I wrote to her. The same sappy and tearful letters I wrote to Jim a few years ago were now directed to Olga.

---

[8] In July 1996, I took all the hand written letters from Olga, typed them up and had them printed in a book entitled *"Letters to Olga"* and gave each Taylor sibling a copy. Most of us love to read and re-read the wonderful stories these letters provided.

A sample of one of them reads:

"Gee, the radio is playing an awful sad song and I'm almost crying while I'm writing to you. I guess it's because I want you back so bad I could cry. Imagine yourself writing to someone you love and hearing a terrible sad song over the radio. Gee, I better stop this because tears are coming to my eyes. Well Goodbye for now. Please write. Take good care of yourself.

Your Sis,

With Love, Kate XXXXXX
PS Write!!

    Obviously, all the weepy movie classics Mom dragged us to see at the Strand, Olympic, Palace, Avon and Town Theaters, like *Wuthering Heights, Gone With The Wind, Lassie Come Home, Casablanca* and all the other tear jerkers, set me up to be the most "blat at the drop of a hat" kid ever to come out of the war era. If Judy Garland and Mickey Rooney had come to Watertown to cast a movie and were looking for a crybaby, I'd be their girl! But thank God, Olga finally came home and for a while I had no more reason to cry over letter-writing, that is until I began writing to a boy who was stationed in Germany.

I was 15 years old at the time and Margaret, at 17, had been dating a guy named Dick[9] who joined the Army and was shipped off to Germany. Dick had a buddy by the name of Bob who hailed from Illinois. Dick suggested to Bob that he should start writing me. So Bob and I began a letter writing campaign that lasted for the rest of my sophomore year and most of my junior year. Finally, I had a real reason to be tearful because I was writing to a boy I so *loved* who was far, far away. Of course, it was insignificant that I was in crying over someone I had never laid eyes on!

The letter-writing became marathon and once again took place to a backdrop of melancholy songs of the day like *Love Is a Many Splendored Thing* and *Unchained Melody*. After many months of correspondence that started out with "It will be great to meet you someday" to "I can't wait to see you" and then "I love you so much, honey," and foolish as this may sound, we eventually talked of marriage and having six kids! And no, I still hadn't even met him.

Finally, Bob wrote to tell me that he was getting out of the Army[10] and his parents were going to drive up to visit family members in Canada. He convinced his parents that they should drop him off at his army buddy Dick's house in Watertown, New York for the summer and of course he and I would finally get to meet.

When I first started writing Bob, he returned my letters to our North Orchard Street address where we had just moved. When he was finally ready to meet me in person, I had to advise him that I was now living on West Lynde Street. Due to the fact that he wouldn't be coming to Watertown for

---

[9] I'm omitting the last names of these guys who can't defend themselves against my crazy memories.
[10] Actually, he told me he was "short". I'm thinking maybe he's warning me that he's about 5' 2" but later he told me that "short" meant soon to be discharged. Whew!

108

another month, I was in constant fear that we might move again and I wouldn't have any way to let him know where to find me.

Just before leaving Germany, he called me for the first time by telephone to tell me when he would be arriving in Watertown. I was shocked when I heard his voice! He sounded to me like Mickey Mouse on helium! Luckily I later found out that it was something about the phone connection and for that I was greatly relieved. The more he talked and sounded like a mouse, the more I was convinced I should tell him I had moved again, but this time, out of state. After all, this would not be shocking considering my past history. I was willing to try anything rather than end up in a permanent relationship with a Disney character. But when I finally laid eyes on him and heard his normal voice and saw that he was pretty dang cute, all fears went away.

On our first date, we went to a drive-in movie theater. Drive-ins were very popular back then and we thought it would give us a great opportunity to talk and get to know each other in a real life situation as opposed to paper and ink. We talked for about ten minutes then watched a movie that today would be labeled a "chick-flick." I chose the sad one (naturally) so we could hug and cry together now that we finally a real live couple. But no tears came and no hugging either. We were two complete strangers and had nothing to say to each other. He took me home, kissed my cheek and told me he'd call the next day.

The next morning I went to the mailbox to get the mail to see if I had a letter from my Soldier Boy. I was disappointed when none was there and it dawned on me that there would be no more letters; he was now home. I wasn't in love with *him* but with the letters and the *thought* of him. I remember feeling pretty let down that this was it. All those letters written under the covers with a flashlight so as not to wake up my roommate, Mom. All that money I spent on sad records to cry to when I thought of him. But Bob realized this as well and we both decided to try to really get to know each other, not just by words on a piece of paper. So the real-life dating began.

At this time, I was working at Netti Wholesale on Bradley Street after school. One day Bob said he would pick me up in the car he had just bought for a few hundred bucks and drive me home. I remember getting out of work and walking towards the car, easy to spot because of its beaten-up body. I found him sleeping with his feet up on the seat and his hat pulled down over his eyes. There was an empty beer bottle on the back seat, a remnant of a party with buddies the night before, and suddenly for some reason he made me think of Dad and Jack all rolled up into one. I almost expected him to sit up, look at me and start extolling the virtues of Super Suds!

He was older than I was; he was out of school, out of the Army and liked to drink beer. It was then that I realized I was really just a kid with another year before I graduated high school. I had never drunk a drop of alcohol, never did anything more than kiss a few boys and had never even gone "steady." What was I thinking? That was the end of our relationship and I went back to dating the geeky high school boys I had thought so immature before.

I must admit that the one good thing I got out of this was I never played a sappy love song while writing a tear-soaked letter again. I guess I grew up when I kissed him goodbye and wished him well as he went back to Elmhurst, Illinois and to his old girlfriend that he then informed me he had been writing to at the same time he was writing me! He even produced her picture from his wallet as a form of proof. She was a lot older than me, quite pretty and looked very worldly. I could picture her smoking cigarettes and driving around in his $400 car while drinking beer with him. They'd probably end up married, have those six kids and she'd wash their clothes with Super Suds. So it was good riddance to my first adventure with love. I did however keep one of his flowery letters for old time's sake. So I got back into being a high school student without a long distance boyfriend to drag me down.

My best friend Marilyn was the schools' best-looking girl, hands down. It was fun to hang around her because the boys were constantly drooling after her. When they realized they couldn't get to her directly, very often they'd come after me with the pretense that it was me they were after. I was wise to the fact that they were using me, but I wasn't stupid. If these hunks wanted to date me on the slim chance that I'd put in a good word to her, that was cool with me.

I have to admit that I loved high school. I wasn't an "A" student because I had absolutely no desire to excel. To me, the whole purpose of high school was to see how much fun you could have, how many tricks you can pull on your friends and to attend as many parties and social events as possible. I've often thought that it's probably just as well that I am not a teenager in this day and age when there's so many more ways to get in trouble.

I just could never refuse a dare. And unfortunately for me but fortunately for my friends, they had but to challenge me to do something they would never do and I was immediately up for it.

In the 9th grade at Holy Family School while supposedly studying with some other students in one of its small side rooms, one of my classmates asked if anyone had heard the new song, "Who Stole the Ding Dong, Who Stole the Bell?"[11] Well I had because music was always playing in our house. So without

---

[11] Written by Dave Mann – hit record sung by Eartha Kitt

111

further ado, I was up *on* the table, belting out the song and doing a dance for everyone. No one let me know that Sister was right behind me watching these antics.

While being subjected to a stern lecture for my "wild behavior unbecoming to a young Catholic schoolgirl," I so desperately wanted to tell Sister that I was this way because of Judy Garland and Stuart Street. It really wasn't my fault, it was Judy's. But alas, I knew Sister wouldn't have understood so I kept quiet and secretly blamed Miss Garland.

I suppose I should have learned that you don't get away with too much in a parochial school but once again as a junior attending Immaculate Heart Academy (IHA), the local catholic high school, I took another dare. This one with more serious consequences.

The old building of the Catholic school was part school and part convent for the Sisters of St. Joseph, the teaching nuns for the local Catholic schools. The wing of the convent that housed the school consisted of many hallways that winded their way in a crazy maze that took such a longtime to navigate. For example, if you were in room eleven and needed to get to room six for your next class, you had to exit the classroom and follow the many twists and turns until you were in another wing that housed the desired classroom. But if you were adventurous enough and brilliant enough, you could see that by climbing out the window from room eleven and entering the outdoor corridor that surrounded both buildings, you could then climb into the window of room six and beat everyone else! How great was this? Why didn't I think of this myself before Marilyn dared me to do it?

Once again I was up for the challenge. And once again I was caught; school uniform hiked up and practically exposing my derriere (sans ugly bloomers at this age,) in a position "very unbecoming to a proper Catholic girl." *How many times would I have to hear that, for Pete's sake?*

Realizing that I couldn't take too many more dressing downs from Mom after the Principal kept calling, I ventured headfirst into being as civic minded and party-minded and pretty much as active a teenage social butterfly as possible. All the while abiding by the school's dictates. A very difficult challenge for me but one I knew necessary in order to graduate and move to New York City with Marilyn as my roommate, splitting our time between all those rich, handsome men.

I tried out for the varsity cheerleading squad and made it on my first attempt. I had cheered during my years at Holy Family elementary so that provided me with some experience. The cheerleaders were required to attend many practices a week plus be at the local games and travel by bus to the out of town games. The buses became a party opportunity on wheels for someone like me. After all, I was the one who had almost never ever seen a sign stating "*You are now leaving the City of Watertown. Come again.*"

Our basketball team was strong and was continuing the legacy of many of the previous tournament-winning teams. The earlier team members consisted of the Doe boys who I had only heard of in passing and certainly I never expected to ever get to meet one, much less marry one.

And for me, the best part was those out of town games. If IHA won an out of town tournament, it was a sure bet that we'd all have our heads hanging out the bus window on our way home, screaming whatever chant was appropriate for that particular win.

"We won the trophy....we won the trophy....we won the Bishop McIntegert trophy....." was the cry that caused me to lose my voice for three days after the tournament. It's amazing how many repetitions of those words you could sing before your voice (and your mind) goes numb.

I dated one of the varsity basketball players during my senior year just because he was the basketball star. He was a junior to my being a senior but he racked up many points each game so he was fun to be seen with after the game at the local soda fountain to sip on cherry cokes. Once the season was gone, so was he.

So here I was, working part time at Netti Wholesale, attending as many parties as I could, trying to at least get my homework done every other night so as not to fail a class, cheerlead at the games, attend the yearbook meetings where I was the book's art editor (go figure – someone had to do it and I could draw a decent straight line), and belonging to the mandatory Marian organization devoted to Our Blessed Mother. I decided I wanted to do more. I became a majorette in the school marching band.

Earlier as a student at Holy Family grade school, some of us girls had the opportunity to learn how to twirl a baton. We attended bi-weekly classes and Mom actually agreed to give me the twenty-five cents for each class to learn how to throw this steel object around. I was never the most dainty person as a teenager so this newly acquired skill of mine not only ended up in my breaking a toe on one occasion and then later spraining my knee, but took out one living room window, two table lamps and one of Mom's religious statues.

It's not enough to just twirl the baton around and around, but you have to learn how to master the moves while jumping in the air and pirouetting around several times. This can be easily accomplished at your local gym or in your back yard. Attempting this while in close proximity to a coffee table in your living room on Curtis Street (or was it

William Street or West Main Street?) can be treacherous.

So now I now had one extra chore at the basketball games. During half time, I'd run into the girl's room, discard my cheerleading uniform of its heavy satin blue and white blouse, and matching long pleated skirt and slip into my majorette costume. I'd hear the band playing *The Star Spangled Banner* as they entered the gym, all the while trying to slip into my even heavier white wool jacket that zipped up the back, weighted down by the royal blue braids and gold cords that hung from each shoulder. The extremely heavy wool skirt, lined in royal blue satin was next. Luckily the blue dyed underpants I wore as a cheerleader were appropriate when I changed into a majorette and saved me a few precious seconds.

Next, the cheerleading white socks and sneakers came off, and the switch to lighter weight socks was made. Finishing off the transformation by stepping into white leather, blue and white tasseled-bearing majorette boots completed the change from "rah-rah" girl to mute twirler. Lastly, I'd place the tall white and blue majorette hat on my head; ruining the hair style I had so painfully pin-curled before the game. Making sure to not forget the most important item of all – my perfect length 30 inch baton, I'd make it to the floor just in time to pull up behind Mary Anne, our head majorette and just in front of Patsy, slightly taller than me. And who said that the players had the toughest job in the game?

The day after the first game where I performed my dual, uniform-switching act, I was called into the Principal's office. Now what, I wondered? I had not jumped up on any table, had not climbed through any window nor had I smoked a forbidden cigarette in the bathroom of the gas station down the street. (At least not this day.) I did not know that Sister Consuella had attended that first game; had witnessed my quick-change act and was worried that the task would be too daunting for me to continue. I sat in the big black leather chair in front of her, studying the swinging, huge rosary beads that fell from her waist and listened while trying to figure out where she was going with this.

""Kathy, I want you to choose one or the other task; either be a cheerleader or a majorette. Doing both is too much for anyone."

I just stared at those beads without saying a word. I had never expected this. I always could juggle anything thrown at me. After all, I was a Taylor. We were never coddled or pampered. If you wanted something bad enough, you broke your back doing it. Gosh, didn't she get this?

"So, which do you want to give up, Dear?" she continued.

Well, that did it. I had just celebrated a whole year of not slobbering in public and now here I was about to go start again. Tears rolling down my face, I just looked at her. She handed me a Kleenex and waited for an answer. There was no way I could choose. I loved both activities. So I decided to tell her just that.

"Sister, will you let me keep doing both and if it doesn't work out, I'll quit one?"

I think she was surprised by my "pluck" or whatever it was, because after a few moments, she smiled and nodded and said,

"Okay, we'll see how it goes. But you be sure to get your rest."

So with that I went back to marathon costume changing and purchased a larger size container of Arrid underarm deodorant to keep both my costumes reasonably dry. I loved all that running back and forth. I was proving I could do just about anything I put my mind too. If only we can take all that teenage adrenalin with us into adulthood! And if only I had placed that same amount of fervor into my studies.

The fact that I never weighed more than 107 pounds during my high school years had a lot to do with my activity level. I kept up this mad switching of ballgame identities through my junior and senior years. Plus the fact that we never had a car to drive us to school and most of the time did not live far enough away to be bused; walking to and from school and practices kept almost everyone in my class at about the same weight. I don't remember any one of us getting rides to Booras's Ice cream Parlor for ice cream sundaes or cherry cokes, and no one would ride a bike – too uncool – so we'd walk to and from those social gatherings. Great for the waistline.

If our ball games were played at home, that would mean walking to the State Armory on Arsenal Street where they were played. And of course during those two years that I cheered and twirled, I lived in about seven different houses, so I was probably a familiar site to almost all of Watertown. I was that skinny kid from IHA walking somewhere all the time with a uniform garment bag tucked over her arm. Most likely I traveled down State Street, Mill Street, Court Street and others, as those streets would empty into Public Square from whatever house we were living in at the time. Then it was just another block or two until I'd be at the State Armory in time to walk through its front doors and into the noise of the boys practicing their pre-game shots. Before your eyes found them, your nose did, taking in the odor of sweaty armpits, way-too-old Ked sneakers and plenty of teen-age testosterone. Oh glorious high school!

In my junior year, at the same time that I was writing to Bob in Germany, I dated a boy named Rich a few times. His family owned a plot of land near their property and often we'd go out back of his house where Rich taught me how to shoot a rifle. We'd shoot at cans and targets tacked to old trees and I actually got pretty good at it. He told me he loved to watch a girl shoot a gun. I think he said that every time I ever went out there target practicing with him. I ended up doing a lot of thinking over that statement.

Rich knew nothing about my writing to Bob from Germany/Illinois and I wasn't about to tell him. But basically Rich and I just had some fun being together and it never got serious. After all, I was still expressing all this pent up puppy-love to my boy in Deutschland.

When the high school prom rolled around, I thought about whom I was hoping would ask me from IHA. Bob and I were a done-deal by then; him having gone back to "what's her name" in Illinois and me trying to put it all out of my mind. Then out of the blue, Rich called and asked if he could take me to the dance. He was attending Watertown High School on the other side of town and it was considered okay to bring someone from a rival school. I was happy he asked me and it took the pressure off wondering if I would get asked by someone from IHA. Besides, he was a nice guy and could afford a nice looking tux.

I then went about trying to acquire the perfect prom dress. Not finding anything in Watertown that made me or my buddy Marilyn happy, we drove to Syracuse in her old beat up car and we shopped for a dress there. I fell in love with a light blue chiffon dress with a full skirt. I picked up a pair of satin shoes and later had them dyed to match the dress. I was all set for the big night. However, I almost did not get to go to my prom at all. At least not with Rich.

About a week before the prom, he stopped over to my house and accidentally learned about my earlier letter-writing affair with Bob. I was home alone and reading a couple of Bob's old letters and trying to decide which single one I would keep for memories' sake before throwing out the rest. I didn't know Rich was coming over and when he came in and saw the bundle of letters at my feet, he picked one up randomly and started reading it. He went rather ballistic! He read words written from some boy in the Army, stating his undying love for me. Rich practically screamed when he read that Bob and I planned on getting married once he got out of the service. I tried to explain that the letters belonged to an *old* boyfriend and I was getting ready to throw them away.

    He didn't believe me and decided he did not want to take someone to the prom that was "'gaga' over some solider boy." His words. So out the door he went with a bang. I ran out front of our house to look for him (I had my gown and shoes hanging in the closet and I needed this date!) but he was gone. I later learned that he had gone up the steps to the second floor landing of the apartment house next door. He was watching me run around the street looking for him so I could convince him that Bob and I were a thing of the past. It took several days of explaining to finally get him to calm down. All this drama for someone I was not in love with and only wanted as a date for the dance. Plus the whole fight started over a guy had no feelings for either. It was all about The Prom!

    Rich and I did end going to the prom and had a very good time. Marilyn and her boyfriend Bill, and Rich and I went to Westcott's Beach afterwards. It was a beautiful night and we were all still dressed up in our finery. I remember it being a full moon that night and the waves were slowly crashing onto shore. We had the beach all to ourselves and Rick put his car radio on full blast. We all took off our shoes and danced in the sand to the background sounds of the waves and to songs like "*Hey There*" by Rosemary Clooney and "*Three Coins in the Fountain*" by The Four Aces.

What fun, dancing barefoot on a beach wearing a pretty, billowy organdy gown on such a gorgeous night! If only I was in the arms of someone who saw me as someone more than Annie Oakley.

Later we threw a beach ball around the sand and then Rich produced a six-pack of beer from the back of his car. Marilyn and I shared one and almost puked! She and I didn't like the way it tasted and I was afraid anyway of getting drunk and possibly start babbling on and on about Super Suds. For all I knew, that's what all people did when they got drunk. I wasn't taking any chances. But I have fond memories of that night which ended up being the last time I went out with Rich.

After graduation I went to work at the New York Telephone Company as a switchboard operator. This was before what was termed "cut-over" which meant that many new employees like me would be losing their jobs. It was a new age of communication technology and we *live* operators would only be needed for long distance assistance. I enjoyed my very decent paycheck while I was there and knew I might only last about two years before I would be laid off. The benefits were good and I often picked a split-shift which was easy to obtain. That meant you would work a few hours in the morning and go home for a while, and come back and work a few more hours in the afternoon. I liked this shift as I could sleep in late, go to work, perhaps to the beach for a few hours and finish off my shift in the early evening. My meeting Dick Doe however, put an end to my career as a telephone operator.

Olga and Bill Sennett's Wedding – 1947
Katherine (left – age 7)
Margaret (right- age 9)

Margaret and Charlie Sexton's Wedding – 1957
In front left to right – Olga and then Katherine.
Dick Doe is 2nd from right in back row
First time meeting for Dick & Katherine

121

**Katherine – 1950 – Age 10
May Crowning**

**Katherine – 1954
Freshman IHA Photo –
Age 14 1/2**

We celebrate our birthday's – 1955 Katherine (age 15) - Margaret (age 17) "Evil" Vernon in background

Mother's Day - 1954
Katherine (Age 14)
Margaret (Age 16)
Mom (age 55)

At IHA, choir members learned the "pose" – stand up straight, hands folded.

Christmas 1955 at Olga and Bill's House

"Evil" Vernon, Katherine, Olga and Margaret

I got to wear Margaret's dress with the fur collar that she wore a year earlier.
(See photo above)

Katherine, Mom and Margaret 1954 –

Sennett's House

Four Youngest Taylor Boys

Vern and Bill in Front
Jim and Tom in Back
Around 1943

THE TAYLOR'S

Family Photo – 1954

Front – Margaret, Olga, Mom and Katherine
Standing – Bill, Jack, Jim, Tom,
Vern and Harvey

Chapter 15

Richard Lawrence Doe

Son of Wilfred C. and Ada Backus Doe

The first Doe to ever grace the shores of North America was Guillaume D'Aoust who was born in France in the 1600's. The D'Aoust family settled in Montreal and many of their offspring eventually made their way across the United States border to settle in Chicago, IL, Buffalo NY, and Ogdensburg, NY. The Doe name began when a descendant, Maurice D'Aoust decided to change it to the easier to pronounce and spell name of Doe. Thank you Maurice from someone who would not want to be known as Katherine D'Aoust!

Maurice Doe and Elmire Sequin Doe had seven children. Wilfred Doe, born in 1905 was known as "John" for most of his life. He had one older sister and five younger brothers. He met and eventually married Ada Backus on November 22, 1926 when he was 21 and she was but 16. They settled in Watertown and a year after their marriage they gave birth to a son named Frederick Charles.

"Freddy" as he was called, died at six months of age from a bowel condition. Three more sons followed in rapid succession, thus John, Richard and Donald were all but two years apart.

Their dad Wilfred was a sports enthusiast of the most serious kind. His boys would learn to play sports and that pretty much was that. Dick remembers being a little tyke when his father decided to teach him and his brother John the game of baseball. In their back yard, their father would position them across from him and pitch the ball to their waiting and homemade little ball mitts. Failure to catch was not really an option. Dick complained once to his father that he was afraid to catch the ball for fear it would hurt. So his father purposely threw the ball right at him hard and said "There...that's as bad as it will be. Didn't kill you, did it?" And that was that.

Fortunately Dick and his two brothers loved sports of any kind. Each son excelled in baseball, basketball, football and later, golf. They were "naturals" as described by local sportswriters. The Doe brothers were famous in the small city of Watertown which boasted a population of about 40,000 at the height of World War II, thanks to the influx of soldiers and their families to Pine Camp (now known as Fort Drum). After the war, the population leveled out to about 30,000 which is pretty much the statistic today.

Money was in short supply in the Doe household, but love was in abundance. Wilfred and Ada spent as much time as they could with their kids and tried in many ways to provide them with enough food on the table and clothes on their back so that they would not feel deprived. They opened a small grocery store in the 1940's and it was rather popular with the people of the neighborhood. It didn't last too long and I have heard that it was mainly because of the generosity of Ada and Wilfred. These were days fresh after the Depression and money was in short supply in most families in Watertown.

When people came in for bread and milk and lunch meat for their kids, credit was readily available, no questions asked. I'm sure there wasn't a person ever turned away hungry by these two generous people. It would have been a miracle if they were able to turn this into a long and successful venture.

But work was not a bad word to Dick's father. He worked in the foundry of a local manufacturing company and later shoveled and delivered coal for a local coal company. "Johnny" Doe would dig a ditch or do anything else that many people would consider beneath them as long as he could hand a check to his beloved Ada at the end of the week. Her job was to stay home and take care of her three boys, a job that she absolutely loved.

The Doe boys were spoiled by their mother. Although the family had no luxuries of any kind, all three boys feel that their mother spoiled them – not with material goods but with love. It was not until they were three or four years old, that the nightly ritual of rocking them to sleep would stop. Most likely the fact that her firstborn son was taken from her at such an early age made her want to smother these remaining sons with all the love she had.

There was never a ball game of any kind, from sandlot ball to grade school on through high school and beyond that didn't feature Wilfred Doe running up and down the sidelines, cheering for the team but most importantly, for his talented sons. How could you not be a successful athlete with the devotion that he placed on his kids? It was never "*if* you win" but "*when* you win." If was never "*try* to do your best"; it was "*you will* do your best." It was a challenge his three sons rose to every time.

The three Doe boys eventually entered the military service after graduating from IHA. Dick had played Red and Black football as soon as he was out of high school and took a sabbatical from the team to do his bit for Uncle Sam. He joined the U.S army in June of 1952 and reported for induction on October 10th of the same year. It wasn't long before he found himself stationed in Korea and was soon in the thick of action on the front lines serving as a Gunner and later as a Squad Leader.

In June of 1953, his squad was asked for volunteers for an especially dangerous mission. Dick volunteered on the spot and listened as an officer described the task ahead of him. Dick was told to write a letter to his parents in the eventuality that he did not return from this risky mission. Dick refused to do so, telling the officer that he had no plans of *not* returning.

What transpired that night is something that Dick described to me only once and then after much prodding and pleading. Nine months after the mission, he was recommended to receive a Bronze Star for his actions and leadership of his squad. The write-up in the Watertown Daily times described it in this way:

Pfc. Richard L. Doe, son of Mr. and Mrs. Wilfred Doe, 204 East Division Street, has been awarded the Bronze Star medal for remaining under fire to relay vital commands to his mortar unit in Korean action.

Private First Class Doe was cited for heroic achievement as a forward observer in the Heavy Mortar Company of the Third Infantry division's 15th regiment near Kang-Chong-Ni last June 14 and 15. Units of the 15th Regiment were defending a strategically located U.N. outpost when Communist forces launched an intense assault against the position.

"During the ensuing fight, many of the enemy soldiers gained the friendly trenches and bunkers. Though surrounded, Doe refused to vacate his post," relates the citation accompanying his award. "He remained on the hill throughout the night, often completely exposed to the intense enemy fire, to relay the necessary fire commands. His actions were highly instrumental in

> the successful defense of the outpost." the citation adds.

The above statement, although highly praising Dick's actions, was virtually stripped of the horrors of the particular mission which awarded him the Bronze Star Medal for Meritorious Achievement. It was a "night from hell" that pinned that medal on his chest, the same medal that he presented to our firstborn son Rick many years later. Dick had no need for medals or prizes or trophies. He knew what he did or did not do in his life. The Bronze Star was stuck away in a drawer until Rick happily claimed it. Throughout his life, the accolades that meant the most to Dick were cards and letters from his three children and the numerous drawings from his grandchildren.

Shortly afterwards, Dick became a sergeant and received a citation for his leadership in that role. The Company Commander who proposed the citation summed it up in this way:

> "Sgt. Doe, serving first as Gunner and later as Squad Leader, performed his duties in a superior manner. His vast technical knowledge of mortar theory and practice was a valuable asset to his unit. He strove long, arduous hours under the most adverse conditions of weather, combat and terrain in order to train the men of his squad in every phase of mortar-infantry tactics. His unwavering determination to complete all missions with the highest standard of efficiency and alacrity constantly evoked the praise of his superiors. As a result of Sgt. Doe's diligent efforts, the men of his

squad were molded into a well coordinated combat team which could be depended upon to provide infantry units with a heavy volume of fast, accurate support fire, which materially sided this regiment in the fulfillment of its mission."

Chapter 16

I Meet the Man I Will Marry

"Be good or I'll give you a black eye"

My sister Margaret had been dating Charlie Sexton for a while and eventually they announced that they planned to be married in July of 1957. Margaret picked my sister Olga for her matron-of-honor and me as her maid-of-honor, and some of her friends as bridesmaids. Charlie's choice for his best man was his brother Tommy Sexton, and one of his ushers was his best friend from high school by the name of Dick Doe. I had never personally met Dick but had certainly heard of his reputation as one of the most talented sports figures in Jefferson County.

As stated earlier, Dick's two brothers, John and Don were equally gifted athletes and their names had graced the local newspapers for years. Anyone that went to either Watertown High School or Immaculate Heart Academy was well aware of the Doe brothers, as was the community at large. Dick was often written up as "diminutive," "powerful, even if small," "little and quick" in articles describing his athletic prowess. He was seen as talent to be reckoned with by all opponents. I remember him being referred to as the "Diminutive Dickie Doe" so often that I wondered how he felt about always having an adjective describing his height as a point of reference.

As I said earlier, in my junior and senior years of IHA I was both a majorette and varsity cheerleader. I later learned that on one occasion Dick and Charlie had attended one of our basketball games. During halftime when we cheerleaders took the floor, Charlie turned to Dick and said "That girl on the right is Margaret's sister." To which Dick is reported to have asked "That skinny one with the ponytail?" I never knew that this was his first impression of me until much later, but I feel I got the ultimate revenge for his snotty remark...I eventually married him.

Margaret and Charlie's wedding was held at Our Lady of the Sacred Heart Church in Watertown. The rehearsal was held the night before and it provided me with my first opportunity to personally meet Dick. I was a little in awe of him because of his reputation and after a few short and pleasant words with him, I went about finding out which guy I would be walking with down the aisle at the wedding. This was important to me because the female attendants were to wear white shoes with 3-inch heels and I wanted to be sure that my 5' 6 ½ " frame would not tower over the guy I would be partnered with. When I was told I was to walk down the aisle with Dick Doe, I was flabbergasted. He couldn't have been more than 5' 6" if he was standing on a stepstool! After much haggling with Margaret, it was decided that I had no say in the matter as many of the other attendants were married or dating and they wanted to be paired up with their significant other. And so it was I would be walking down the aisle with the "Diminutive Dickie Doe."

The wedding was very nice and the reception was held at the Italian American Club. When it came time for all the paired attendants to take to the dance floor together, I remember at first feeling foolish towering over Dick but I eventually kicked off my shoes and found out that and inch or so wasn't that big a deal. He was a great jitter-bugger and we had a really good time.

Later on, word went around that some of the wedding attendants were heading to Morgia's Beach after the reception. It was a hot night and everyone was exhausted from the marathon dancing and partying, and so going would give us a chance to cool off. It sounded like a lot of fun to me so I went over to my mother's table to tell her where I was going and who with. She definitely was not excited about my going out so late at night but I had just graduated from high school and would soon be eighteen so she had recently started letting me have a little more freedom.

Dutifully, she told me to be careful and expressed her concern that "Some of those guys are a lot older than you, and that fellow Dick Doe is almost 25 years old." I calmed her fears by telling her I was not the least bit interested in him or anyone in the party and because the reception was almost over, we just wanted to go swimming to cool off. I promised not to be late, and after we all stopped at our respective houses for bathing suits and towels, we were off to the beach.

It was a beautiful night and the guys put their car radios on full blast and brought out beer for everyone. I was not old enough to drink and still not interested in it, so I grabbed one of the soft drinks that they also brought, albeit only a few. Soon everyone was really having a blast. Water fights began and couples were vying to see who could be the winners. Each guy hoisted a gal on his shoulders and the gals on top would pummel each other until the loser ended up in the water. I climbed up on Dick's shoulders ready to fight but immediately lost balance and fell off. Dick took another breath and went under so I could get back on again. At that moment, I bent down to take some seaweed out of my toes and because Dick couldn't stay under the water any longer, he came charging back up to the surface for air, vigorously shaking the water out of his hair and hitting me square over my left eye! Instantly I could feel my eye puff up and close. Dick was extremely apologetic but all I wanted was to get out of the water and check out my throbbing eye.

I walked up to one of the parked cars and looking into its side mirror thought, "Oh my gosh, how am I going to explain this to Mom?" We stayed at the beach until close to midnight and then everyone started for home. Dick offered to drop me off at my house and once again told me how sorry he was. I wasn't worried about how my eye felt as much as what Mom would say when she took a look at me.

In keeping with her past practice, Mom came out of her bedroom when she heard me come home. I told her we had a good time and that I was going to bed, all the while not looking at her. I thought perhaps it wouldn't look so bad in the morning. Wrong! I awoke to the aching pain over my eye and went to the bathroom to take a better look at the source of all this agony. I took one look in the mirror and couldn't believe what I saw! My eye was practically closed but the color is what was so noticeable. It was yellow, purple, green and in general, just a mess. There would be no hiding it from Mom and when I went to the kitchen to get something for breakfast, I heard her coming out of her bedroom. I turned to look at her and immediately said, "Let me explain...."

More than anything I had to convince her that this 25 year old "older man" had not bopped me in the face on purpose. She finally accepted my explanation but for years I had to listen as Dick teasingly told everyone that I got fresh with him on our first date and he had to defend his honor!

My eye finally healed and Dick called to inquire as to how it was and to ask if I would want to go out to a drive-in movie? We began dating and it was comfortable, but no sparks flew. He would take me over to his house and because his mother was such a fantastic cook, it was my favorite date. We'd sit on the couch and eat her chocolate brownies topped off with a huge bowl of popcorn and watch television, still in its prime, and mostly broadcasting

Milton Berle and Ed Sullivan shows, mixed in with some quality movies of the week.

    A few months later Dick was again an usher in his good friend Budgo's wedding. As we were still dating quite steadily, I attended as Dick's guest. We danced a lot that evening at the reception and had a great time. Later on, for some reason that I can't recall, we got into a small argument that escalated until he went outside to cool off. I had planned to spend the evening at Margaret and Charlie's house that night so I got a ride there even though they were staying a while longer at the reception. I was sitting on their living room couch watching TV when Dick called on the phone, telling me he would like to come up and see me and apologize. He did come up and after everything was smoothed over and we were back on speaking terms, it was then that he told me that he loved me and realized it when it bothered him that we had a disagreement. Thus our relationship went to a new level. Now instead of seeing each other most of the time, it was now all of the time.

    I was making a pretty decent paycheck working at the New York Telephone company as a switchboard operator when dating Dick. I was scheduled to work on my 18th birthday which also coincided with New Year's Eve. Dick had assumed that we would go out to celebrate this festive night and also this special birthday of mine. I would finally be an adult and he wouldn't feel like he was robbing the cradle. My schedule called for me to go into work at 11:00 pm, just when the night would start to get interesting. Because I had only worked there for eight months, I had no seniority and could not get out of working this shift, no matter how hard I tried. Unbelievably, I chose to quit my job rather than lose out on my night with Dick. I say unbelievably because the job was such a good one, good wages and benefits. But at eighteen, your heart usually rules your head. After our fun night out with mutual friends, I took a job as a secretary at a local furniture store at a big decrease in salary. That would teach the telephone company for trying to ruin my birthday!

    Dick had a ton of friends, some married and some not. Parties and get-togethers several times a month were the norm. Meeting at local bars after a sports event was where you met all your mutual friends and everyone got along so well. Dick was playing Red and Black football at the time and was a very popular star of the team. I reveled in being on his arm after the games when fans would come up to congratulate him on his playing and a few times even local sports writers would catch him to get a few quotes for the next days report. We seemed to be in a whirlwind of games, parties, friends, his family get-togethers and just generally had a wonderful courtship.

    One day many years later, I explained to my daughter the way we spent our holiday celebrations back when her parents were dating and then right after we were married. There was no going out to fancy nightclubs or staying all night in expensive hotels and partying until dawn as is popular to do today. But buying a beautiful dress, heels and jewelry was important. It's funny to think now of the money I'd try to get together in order to have a lovely satin or organdy dress, matching shoes and rhinestone earrings in order to visit a friend's house for New Year's Eve. But that's how it usually went. There would be about eight or nine couples invited. We'd all get our kids to bed, say goodbye to the sitter and go out about nine in the evening. The gals would usually gather in one room and the guys in the other but eventually we'd all get together for dancing, drinking, eating, perhaps a game of some sort and then the inevitable noise makers at the stroke of midnight. Every guy kissed his and every other guy's wife. There would be much merry making and then a few hours later, we'd all head for home. I have seen photos and even films of these occasions and it makes me smile to remember how much fun we all had on these simple occasions. Simple that is except as I said earlier, for the dresses. At one party I wore a blue satin dress and at another, a red organdy and tulle dress. These usually had the required crinoline slips underneath and were, in my eyes, a thing of beauty. It's hard to imagine anyone getting all dressed up like that today to go out for a holiday party at someone's house. Perhaps a dress pair of slacks and nice sweater, but that would be about it.

    Dick did not have a flair for the romantic even though he definitely *was* very romantic. A case in point is the way in which I received my engagement ring. Very often on a warm summer night we'd catch a new movie at the Black River Drive-in. His mother would pack up some goodies, we'd grab soft drinks and off we'd go to catch a double feature. It was an opportunity for us to do some talking before the movies started and a lot of kissing and hand holding when it was going on.

    On one particular night in April, we were heading out of his house to get in his car to go to the drive-in. His mother was standing in the front yard looking rather sheepish. Dick said to me "Oh Gaff[12], would you do me a favor and grab me a handkerchief from my top dresser drawer in my bedroom?" I thought it was odd that he asked me this since he had just left his bedroom to grab his wallet. But I dutifully went in, opened the small top drawer which was loaded with white handkerchiefs, grabbed the first one I saw and went out to hand it to him. He and his mother just smiled and looked at me strangely. I asked them what was so funny. Then

---

[12] Dick used to call me "Kath" and one day yelled "Hey Gaff" by mistake. I became "Gaff" to him then and he still uses it to this day.

Dick asked me to go back and get another one from the same drawer. At this point I'm a bit upset, but back in I went and this time when I grabbed a handkerchief, I felt something solid under it. I discovered it was a box and I knew immediately that it was a ring box. So here I am, all alone in my boyfriend's bedroom, in his "snot-rag" drawer, opening up a box containing my engagement ring! Only Dick! I took one look at the solitaire diamond and couldn't believe he had purchased such a beautiful ring on his own. I had always thought that I would have a part in choosing my own engagement ring but Dick obviously had other plans.

I went screaming and running out of the house and onto the front porch and looking down at the ground where Dick stood grinning from ear to ear. I jumped into his arms, almost knocking him over and he knew what my answer was. We hadn't talked about marriage specifically but I think we both knew it was certainly a strong possibility. Less than two years after Margaret and Charlie's wedding, I walked once again down the aisle of Our Lady of the Sacred Heart Church but this time to the waiting arms of the "Diminutive Dickie Doe."

OUR WEDDING DAY – MAY 16, 1959

Front Row – L to R
Cheryl Taylor (My brother Bill's daughter) - Flower Girl
- Danny Taylor (My brother Jim's Son) – Ring Bearer
Margaret (Taylor) Sexton,
Nancy (Kissel) Maurer,
June (Bush) Alteri, Brenda Armstrong

Second Row – Katherine, Dick, Don Doe,
Jim Powell, John Ramus,
Olga (Taylor) Sennett, Donna Taylor,
Junior Bridesmaid

Rear – Charlie Sexton, Budgo Alteri, John Doe

Honeymooning at Cooperstown Baseball Hall of Fame – 1957
I'm on Ted William's Bench
Yipee!

Chapter 17

Introducing Mr. and Mrs. Richard L. Doe

"Do you take this man for better or for worse...and will you love him even if he takes you to the Baseball Hall of Fame on your honeymoon?"

So I'm sitting on Babe Ruth's bench while visiting Cooperstown, New York on my honeymoon. This should have been a clue! I should have known this would be a precursor to a life of sitting on benches at baseball games, softball games, basketball games, football games, or standing in the sidelines at golf games, horseshoe games, or anything that ended in "games." But on my honeymoon?

We had a wonderful wedding on May 16, 1959. I was only 19 years old and Dick a much older 26. Margaret and Charlie returned the favor by standing up for us as did my sister Olga, Dick's two brothers John and Don, my niece Donna Lee Taylor and some of our best friends. The wedding party including Dick and I, totaled 16 people. The reception was held at the Italian-American Club and more than 250 friends and family members attended and danced to a band that set us back more than fifty bucks, a ton of money to us back then. Dick's parents gave us $200.00 as a gift and we decided we would "blow every darn cent of it on our honeymoon." We knew it would be a long time before we ever had that much cash all at once again. Our furniture had already been purchased and was securely ensconced in our adorable rented dollhouse on the corner of LeRay Street and West Lynde Street. The only disagreement we had during the engagement was deciding on where we would go on our honeymoon.

Dick had been playing that spring on a baseball team sponsored by a local restaurant...all right, a bar. Anyway, I told him that his games would just have to proceed without him as we were going away for a whole week, Saturday to Saturday. He agreed on the timeline and after a lot of discussion, he suggested that we should see a lot of New York State.

"You know, travel around, Gaff, and really get to know the state we live in."

So that's how I ended up sitting on Ty Cobb and Babe Ruth's bench; posing next to Lou Gehring's uniform; smiling beneath photos of Cy Young and Walter Perry Johnson. I didn't know this was his planned destination as he drove me immediately out of town heading straight to Cooperstown where I spent two "forgettable" days.

Recently I came across those photos of me, so innocent, so unaware of the life I'd live as a "sport's widow." My eyes were lit up waiting for my new husband to press the shutter on our Polaroid camera, purchased just for the occasion.

No sooner than he'd take and process the first photo, then he would instruct me to "Go sit over there Gaff, on the same bench that the 'Babe' sat on. Isn't that neat? Isn't this great? Isn't this different?"

"*Yup*," I drawled just like Lou Gehring would, "*This here shore is different, Dick.*"

I specifically remember attending Mass on the day after our wedding because of what happened as I proceeded up to the communion rail for the first time as a married woman. This was in the days of nylon stockings, the kind that came in pairs, as in two, one for each leg. Consequently they had to be held up by something and a garter belt was in every young woman's lingerie drawer. I was wearing my new beige and avocado green linen dress, purchased just for our honeymoon. Of course this was topped with a matching avocado pillbox hat and I looked damned cute. So while in the small church we had discovered close to our hotel, I stood up for the gospel reading and felt something under the back of my dress give way. Instantly I could tell that it was the snap from the garter belt. I couldn't believe what I was feeling - the sensations of my nylon stockings slowly creeping down my legs.

Thankfully it was time to sit back down for the homily and I never heard a word that the priest said as I pondered on what my next move would be. I had no idea where the restroom was as we were in some hick town just outside of 'Baseball Bat City,' so I managed to use my elbows to ride the belt up to where I felt it should be. I was mildly successful and had the feeling that it would remain in this position until we left church but I began worrying about what would happen when it was time to walk up the aisle to receive communion.

Before I had much time to contemplate this, the man to my right was signaling for me to leave the pew and head up to the altar. That's when everything north started heading south. I held my arms locked to my sides, thinking I had the garter belt under control but in reality, I was just holding up my slip, which needed no assistance. After I received communion and on my way back down the aisle heading for our pew, the belt was now down to my knees and I was walking like a wounded nurse just home from the Korean conflict. I waddled straight out the back door, leaving my new husband in complete bewilderment as to why this supposedly good Catholic girl was not even staying put until the end of Mass.

Dick followed me and watched in bewilderment as I quickly approached the car, got in, stripped off the nylons and garter belt and tossed the garments into the back seat. He stood outside the opened door of our 1954 Chevy trying to figure out this strange behavior on the part of a girl who had previously been very virginally shy and I suspect he was pretty excited about my newfound wanton ways. He quickly jumped into the car with anticipation on his greedy little face wondering what I was about to do next. After I explained the reasons for my bizarre actions to him, we both laughed all the way back to our hotel where he took advantage of his brazen and stocking-less new bride.

The next day after touring Howe's Taverns where I happily rode an elevator that quickly descended forty stories into the ground[13], we headed out to visit with Margaret and Charlie and their baby daughter Laura. The Sexton's were now living in Cortland, NY where Charlie was working for Niagara Mohawk. Their house was cute but small and the only extra bed they had was in the crowded nursery. So we spent the third night of our honeymoon nestled in a single bed in Laura's room, trying to smooch without waking up the baby. We may have been close in proximity to the Pocono's, but this *wasn't* the Pocono's. No heart-shaped bed and tub here. Just a small crib and a snoring baby three feet away.

After leaving the Sexton's house, we traveled a bit more around different cities and then on Wednesday while out to dinner, Dick nervously told me he had something to ask me. Here it was, the watermark of our future existence as a couple...

"Could we possibly go home earlier than planned Gaff, so I could play in Thursday night's really, really important ballgame?"

---

[13] It's hard to imagine this today as I am terrified of elevators. About 5 years ago I found a free pass issued to us by Howe's while on our honeymoon. It stated that if we ever came back to the caverns we'd have a free admission pass to go underground again. No thank you!

I thought for a while and more or less decided "What to hell?" I was living a sports honeymoon with a sports fanatic who talked and thought sports even with his new bride so we might as well go back so he can actually play the game. So we packed up, headed for home and surprised no one when he ran out and onto the field with his ball uniform on, his glove firmly placed on his left hand and a brand new gleam in his eye. His team won that night.

We quickly settled into the routine of Mr. and Mrs., while at the time we were both working at New York Air Brake Company and unfortunately in the same department. I say unfortunately because working with your husband, even though newly married, can be a bit too much. At first it was kind of fun and different but I worried that it might become a problem. I was very happy when I found out one month after our wedding, that I was pregnant. I had never planned to be a working mother anyway, so I gave my notice when I was in my third month. I was so ill with morning sickness for the first four months that it was a joy to be able to barf in my own bathroom instead of the Air Brake's.

Dick and I looked forward to parenthood with a real fervor. I would pack his lunch each morning and put little love notes in it and signed "Love, Gaff and 4/9's Ricky" or "5/9's Ricky" depending on the extent of my pregnancy. We were sure it would be a boy and we would name him Richard but call him Ricky. There were no pregnancy test kits back then and my obstetrician never made anything but a slight guess about the sex of the baby so as to not disappoint the parents.

Chapter 18

Lisa Marie Doe
Born April 28, 1960

"Ricky, you look like a little girl"

"Ricky" was born on April 28, 1960 and the only surprise was that *he* was a *she*. We looked at this 7 pound, 2 oz. dark haired beauty and couldn't figure out what had happened. We felt we were fooled in some way but were delighted with the results. We named her Lisa Marie and she was absolutely the best baby a mother could ask for. She slept through the night at 3 weeks which made me the envy of my friends who had infants who still awoke for nighttime feedings long after that.

I loved being a stay-at-home Mom and really didn't have friends who were not also staying at home with their new babies. I recently heard someone describe the job of a stay-at-home mother as having the world's most important job...that of *raising human beings.* That's the way I felt and I loved it. I'd do my laundry or ironing with Lisa right by my side and the radio on, listening to my favorite soap operas. I had a little nip-nap carrier and I'd take her with me from room to room if she wasn't napping. I was such a young mother at 20 that it was as if I was playing house. I almost looked forward to her spitting up on one of her cute little dresses as this gave me an opportunity to change her into another one. I'd wash and iron her pretty clothes and hang them on little teeny hangers on the back of our bedroom door and would take several minutes making the decision on which color she would wear that day. I was a happy camper and the world seemed perfect.

Lisa was so small and petite, that she caused a lot of surprised reactions when she decided to walk. I played with her almost non-stop from morning to night. I treated her like a doll and decided I wanted to have her walk very young. At seven months of age, I had her balancing herself in our living room for up to a minute or two, and at eight months she'd take a few steps into my waiting arms. It was no surprise to me that she took off walking across the room on the day she turned ten months old.

During this time Dick was working a few nights a week at the Watertown Bowl, a local bowling establishment and restaurant. He was a bartender and a pretty good one. Being a Doe meant that you had plenty of opportunities to learn about different 'beverages'.

One night I drove out to the Bowl with Lisa in tow. We visited her father and had a bite to eat. She was wearing an adorable white and pink pinafore dress and shiny white Mary-Jane shoes. She was getting antsy and wanted to get down from my arms so I let her down. Watching this teeny, bitty ten-month old creature run full speed ahead surprised so many patrons that some of their jaws dropped. Lisa was the size of a large doll and was wearing a size 6 month dress when she was ten months old so you can imagine how small she appeared.

I know a great many mothers who will say that their child was almost perfect. I know what they mean because as a baby, a toddler and later an adolescent and teen, Lisa gave me about a handful of problems and that was all. She just was a child that did not want to disobey, was easy to please, happy and just delightful to be around. I don't ever remember her defying any order we gave her or her challenging any house rule. Except of course, for the time that her actions resulted in the famous "bicycle in the bedroom punishment." I may have the "pickle juice story" as part of my legend but Lisa has the "bicycle in the bedroom" story as part of hers.

    Our house on Cooper Street was well known as the neighborhood hangout. Dick and I always preferred for our kid's friends to come to our house where we could keep better watch over our own kids. Lisa began the tradition and later Rick and Mike kept it going. There was almost never a weekend night that our front yard was not covered by kids of all ages. When they were small, Lisa's friends were of the same gender. Later she and her best friend Kathy Vespa grew to be both cute and popular so there was never a shortage of boys on our front porch, showing off for the two of them.

    But I can honestly say that there was not one kid that hung around our house that I didn't love. They were a great bunch, most of them from the neighborhood at large and later, our kid's best friends from school. As little kids, the games were played out front of our house. Games like Kick the Can, Movie Star, Hide and Go Seek and even Hot Beans and Butter. (More on this last game later). As the kids grew in age, the games took on more of intensity. Hide and Go Seek was a serious game and therefore you had to plan where you would hide very calculatingly because to be "It" was not as much fun as being the one searched for.

    Our poor neighbors had to deal for years with kids hiding in their bushes, in and under their porches and if it were possible, they would have opened their doors to cower in their hallways. Because there were so many kids around our house for so many years, eventually their bicycles ended up being sprawled all over our lawns and the lawns of our very patient neighbors, Werner and Virginia Steinaker. They never complained but I'm sure they were happy when our kids left home and their lawns could resume growing.

If our kid's and their friend's bikes were not on the lawn, they were in our driveway. It absolutely infuriated Dick to come home, expecting to drive his car into the driveway and find five or ten or even more bikes casually thrown across the blacktop or across our neighbor's lawn. We worked hard on getting the visiting kids to obey the rule, but for some reason, they just didn't get it. It seemed that Lisa's friends were the worst offenders and her own bike on more than one occasion would be sprawled right at the entrance to the driveway, a fact that Dick decided one night to remedy.

Pulling himself up to his five foot, six inch height, he declared to her at dinner one night that one more occurrence of his finding her bike in the driveway would result in her having to sleep with it in her bedroom! Of course there were snickers all around the table. Who in their right mind would actually carry that silly threat out? Dick Doe, that's who?

About a week later Dick came home and there was Lisa's Schwinn blocking the entrance to the driveway. I *heard* Dick before I saw him, huffing and puffing as he carried something up the stairs, cussing all the way. I followed him up just in time to watch him place the bike at the foot of Lisa's bed with a flourish.

"There, that will teach her. That bike stays there for a week!"

"You're not serious are you, Dick?"

"Yes I am and I'll bet it won't happen again."

When Lisa came in for dinner, her father said nothing about the bike. When she ran up the stairs to get something a while later, we could hear her laughing and down the stairs she bound, ready to have a good laugh with her father. But quickly she realized that he was dead serious. He informed her that it would stay there for one week and he finished by saying that he was sure that the next time she

149

thought about parking her bike, it would be off the driveway and off the neighbor's lawn. And it was. I can only imagine the discomfort of having to dress and move around a 9 x 12 bedroom with an adult sized 10-speed bike in the way.

    I think Lisa learned her lesson as to this very day she doesn't park her car on her and her husband David's lawn or their neighbors.

Chapter 19

Susan Kathleen Doe

Born and Died September 13, 1961

When Lisa was about six months old, a new complex called Cloverdale Apartments was built in Watertown. This was the first of subsidized housing and we were told this meant that we could live in one of these cute two-bedroom apartments for less than we were currently paying. In that way we could save money to purchase our own home. We decided to leave our LeRay Street apartment and make the move.
    Not long after we unpacked, I received a call from the New York Air Brake Company wanting to know if I could fill in on a temporary job. Dick and I discussed this long and hard and as long as Dick's mother was willing to take care of Lisa for a few months, I would take the position so we could more quickly acquire the down payment for our own home. So back to work I went and just after Lisa's first birthday, we had enough money to put down on a large house on Cooper Street, a house that we would live in for the next forty years. Everything was according to our plan, or so we thought.
    Dick and I discovered that we were expecting another baby and it came as a slight surprise. We knew we wanted more children but hadn't even discussed it when I became sick in the mornings and knew instantly what was causing it. We were to have a baby in December of '61 and because we knew we could use a little more money before I was home with two small children, it was decided that I would continue to work until my sixth month of pregnancy.

September 13th was like any other day. I woke early, fed and dressed Lisa, ate breakfast with Dick, got dressed and ready to ride together to work. First we stopped at my mother-in-law's house where Lisa eagerly ran to her Grandmother's waiting arms. With my mother-in-law, we never had to worry about leaving her with someone who loved her any less than we did. Dick's mother was and is a gem. She not only took wonderful care of Lisa but when we went to pick her up at 4:30 each day, Grandma would very often have dinner waiting for us. We'd sit down to a huge meal of potatoes, meat, freshly cooked vegetables, rolls, pies and cakes. On many occasions, I would drop our laundry off and she'd iron and starch Dick's shirts and my blouses and dresses. She loved doing it and we'd give her a few extra dollars for it along with the little pittance she would take from us for watching Lisa. She would have preferred to accept no pay but we forced her to take something.

    I was working in the Engineering department of the New York Air Brake as a secretary. I remember September 13th very well, sitting in my comfortable chair, engrossed in typing a long proposal for my boss. I was suddenly aware that the cushioned chair was wet, and thinking I was having a weak bladder moment; something all pregnant women can relate to, I got up and rushed to the ladies restroom. Then the damn burst. My water broke as I entered the room and I don't think I still had any real idea of what had just happened. An older female co-worker happened in just as I was surveying the back of my water-stained dress. She immediately knew what was wrong and encouraged me to go home at once. I left and went to get my purse and explain to my boss, embarrassingly – this was the 60's after all – that I must go home. I then placed a call to Dick in the adjoining Publications Department and he came and drove me to our

Cooper Street house. One call to my doctor and the next thing I knew I was in the hospital awaiting birth of a baby that was three months too early.

I was surprised at how intense my labor was. I had mistakenly thought if you were not a full nine month's pregnant, then perhaps the pain would not be so strong. I quickly found out that the contractions are not related to the baby's size. Their intensity increased and it became apparent that they would not stop as we had hoped. The nursing staff was very animated and nervous waiting for the doctor to arrive. Before he did, I had profuse bleeding and I was sure I was about to die. I can close my eyes today and still see the sheets becoming bright red all around my body. There were about ten people in my small room and the flurry of activity was hectic. Suddenly I was wheeled into the operating room and thankfully my doctor arrived. He told me that he did not have good news; that the baby was about to be born and way too early. He said he suspected placenta previa[14] as the cause and went on to tell me that the baby would be very small and not likely to survive.

I saw an ether mask come over my face and the next thing I knew, I was in the recovery room and the nurse was attempting to open my clenched hand and remove the Miraculous Medal of Our Blessed Mother that had been given to me by Mom many hours earlier. I had been holding on to it so tightly that there was an imprint of the medal in my palm for many hours later. The doctor entered my room and when I asked him how the baby was, he sadly told me that it had been a girl weighing only one pound and one ounce and had expired an hour after birth. I don't remember feeling anything but numb.

---

[14] Placenta previa is an obstetric complication that occurs in the second and third trimesters of pregnancy. It may cause serious morbidity and mortality to both fetus and mother. It is one of the leading causes of vaginal bleeding in the second and third trimesters. (From www.eMedicine.com)

It did not dawn on me for days what has just occurred. I felt too immature to have had such a traumatic thing happen at the young age of 21.

    The nurse asked me to sign some papers and when I looked at the certificate, I was surprised to see a name for the baby - Susan Kathleen. I asked her where that name had come from and she told me I had given it when prompted in the recovery room. Dick and I had never settled on a name. Because once again we had no way of knowing the sex of our unborn child and because we had thrown many names around thinking we still had three months to go, we had settled on nothing definite. The only reasonable explanation I had was that my sister Olga had always wanted a baby girl after the birth of her son Mark. She had many times said that she would have named her Susan Kathleen. She liked the name Susan as a first name and would use Kathleen as the middle name. The name Kathleen would be in honor of our sister who died in her first year of life.

    I accepted the fact that I must have been the one to give the nurse this name. Otherwise how could the hospital staff come up with it? And it was indeed a lovely name so it remained. When Olga found out the name I had given our daughter, I'm sure she must have wondered why I did that. As I said, I had no intention of doing so but she became and is, our daughter Susan Kathleen Doe. I like to think that my big sister named her for us.

Chapter 20

Richard James Doe
April 22, 1964

Finally - - a "Ricky"!

Dick and I made a concerted effort to not get pregnant again for a few years so that I could regain my health. I had some problems after Susan's birth but finally got strong again so when we found out we were expecting again in the latter part of '63, we were ready and hoping to provide Lisa with a little brother. Maybe we'd have little Ricky after all.

This birth was not expected to take place until May 13th or so and in fact we had hoped it might happen on our wedding anniversary which was May 16th. But in April I had contractions on a daily basis and my doctor told me that these were Braxton-Hicks contractions which can be a blessing as my labor should be quicker when I was ready to give birth. He didn't know how right he would be!

I awoke early on the morning of the April 22nd, five o'clock to be exact. What woke me up was that these contractions were much more serious from what I had previously experienced. I was still sure they were not the type that would take me into labor so I lay in bed trying to work my way through them. A few minutes later I got up and went into the bathroom to get a drink of water and think this pain thing over. It was while there that I realized that this was a lot more serious than Braxton-Hicks. This was the real thing even though it was three weeks ahead of schedule.

Because I wanted to look nice when I went to the hospital, it was with legs crossed and panting heavily that I applied my makeup. I made sure that I put on blue eye shadow to match the blue and white outfit I would wear to the hospital. Soon I realized that things were moving very speedily and I needed to wake up Dick to have him take Lisa to his mother's house. I kissed our daughter goodbye and promised her a baby that day and as soon as she and her father were gone, I finished curling my hair and applying my lipstick. One had to look very nice when giving birth. When Dick returned I informed him that it was definitely time to head for the hospital.

Our ride that morning through the early off-to-work traffic was nothing short of a "Lucy and Ricky" episode. I had to stand as straight up as I could in the front seat of the car as Dick took each corner on two wheels. He honked the horn all the way around Public Square and was way over the speed limit. He told me later that when he passed the policeman on the America Corner heading towards the hospital, the cop just waved him on, obviously knowing full well where we were headed. I suppose not too many women rode past him standing upright in the car!

Amazingly I was able to walk into the hospital and into the Admissions Office. I could not sit down and informed the receptionist of that fact. She called for a wheelchair and in about a minute I was saying goodbye to my husband as he finished the necessary paperwork. His last words to me were "I'll be right up in a minute. You go get settled in."

By the time Dick finished signing forms and headed for the elevator, I was on the delivery table. Talk about fast! As soon as I had made it to the 2nd floor Maternity Ward, the contractions came crashing down one after the other. The nurse who was waiting for me took one look and her experienced eyes knew it wouldn't be long. Almost in an instant, I was in a hospital gown and on the table, an ether cone coming down over my nose and it was lights out for me.

At about this same time, Dick had exited the elevator and headed for the desk on the Maternity Ward. A nurse came to him to ask him if he were Mr. Doe. Affirming that he was, he asked where the waiting room was so he could get settled in to await the birth of his child.

"Well, we were looking for you Mr. Doe, you have a baby boy," was the smiling nurse's next words.

"No, I don't think so," my astonished husband said. "My wife just got here about ten minutes ago. I've been downstairs signing forms."

"Well, I'm telling you," the nurse continued, "she gave birth very fast and it's all over."

When I woke up a short while later, I was aware of my face being washed clear and void of all my colorful makeup. An older nurse had made the decision that I didn't need that blue eye shadow. If she only knew the pain behind each stroke of the shadow brush hours earlier. But it was all so worth it. We finally had our Ricky. I definitely felt like Lucy Ricardo.

Lisa was very excited to learn that she had a baby brother. She could not wait for him to come home but she needed to be patient because back in the 1960's, new mothers spent an average of 5 or 6 days on the maternity floor, waiting to get our "strength back."

Finally our son did come home with us and right into the waiting lap of his four year old sister. She had always loved playing Mommy to her various dolls and we knew she would take to the task of being a big sister eagerly. But what she hadn't counted on was the baby's cry...long and lusty sometimes.

On the second day of our son living in our home, I was changing his clothes in the downstairs den and he was hungry and howling at the top of his lungs. I tried to soothe him and out of the corner of my eye, I could see Lisa placing her hands over both of her ears and moving further and further away from this screaming, red-faced, scrunched up little person. The next thing I knew, I heard the front screen door close and could tell she had exited the house. Scooping up the baby in my arms, I went to see where she was and saw her running down the street yelling "I don't want him to cry – make him stop!" So much for the big sister act. I took her a while to realize that all babies acted that way and she eventually warmed up to the idea of being his big sister, wails and all.

Rick was a handsome baby. I remember one time when he was about a year old and I had him at the pediatrician's office for a checkup. He was sitting on the table, all dressed in an adorable green outfit with a little matching cap. His hair was rather long and dark and wavy. The doctor said "You know Kathy, this is one good looking boy. I predict he'll be a lady killer in his teens." I made a mental note to enter that into his baby book when I went home. He might need that quote someday.

He too was a good baby, sleeping all night long very early on once he got to sleep. I say "once he got to sleep" because many nights when I would lay him down in his crib and started to walk away, he would be aware that I was leaving and start to howl. So on a good many nights I'd rub his back until he fell off to sleep. I hated the squeaky stairs that gave me away as I tried to sneak back down. One loud creak and he'd demand another back rub. This went on for way too many nights for me not to remember even today.

Chapter 21

Michael Andrew Doe

October 2, 1965

So now that we had an adorable daughter and a handsome son, all was well in our world. When Rick was eight months old and happily crawling all over the furniture, lovingly watched by his big sister, now five years old, I caught a stomach bug that turned out to be named Michael Andrew. I was sure that's all it was when I became extremely ill for four mornings in a row. On the 5th morning, it dawned on me that this might be not a bug but a pregnancy. I was right and so was my mother. She had come over that morning to visit, took one look at me and said "Katherine, I can tell by your eyes that you're going to have a baby." (She may have said that or else "you're in the family way" but never "pregnant" – God forbid she would ever use that term). I had to concur with her at this point and a visit to the doctor a few days later confirmed it.

Once again my body could not seem to wait the usual nine months to give birth and when I started serious contractions a good three and a half weeks early, we decided not to wait until the last minute like we did for Rick. We called Dick's mother and she came over to stay with Lisa and Rick and close to midnight on the 1st of October, we headed for the hospital. Probably because he wasn't quite ready to leave the comfort of his mother's womb so early, Michael kept me in labor for eighteen hours.

On the afternoon of October 2, 1965, all 5 pounds, 14 ounces of him came wailing into the world. I remember calling my sister Margaret in Cortland later in the day to tell her she was an aunt again. At that very moment, she was hosting a birthday party for her son Robbie's 4th birthday and I told her to tell him that Aunt Katherine had a nice little "cousin birthday present" for him.[15] I found it more than coincidental that Jackie Jr. was my birthday present many years earlier and now Robb too had a birthday present in the form of a cousin. We Taylor's were big on gifting relatives with babies.

Michael Andrew was so small that I was afraid he would break. His little arms and legs were very scrawny and frail looking. I had told someone that he reminded me of a little chicken and they and I had laughed. A few days later I had made the same statement to someone else and to this day can see the fire in Dick's eyes when he heard me say that again about his newborn son. He looked straight at me and pointing his finger in my face said to me "Don't you *ever* refer to Michael as a chicken again. He is my son and does *not* look like a chicken!" I never did that again, I promise you. And anyway, he grew faster than his sister and brother did and filled out very quickly and in a matter of a few more weeks looked more like a fat bantam rooster.

If I do not say here that Mike was another wonderful baby that slept all night and gave me no trouble, it is not because I forgot to mention it. It's because it would not be true. This kid was nothing like his siblings. He was born with a fire in his belly and it appeared that he could not wait to start each day to see what mischief he could get into. Margaret told me over and over again that his being born on Robb's birthday meant Mike would have the same spirit as his cousin and that was so true.

I easily remember how sad it was for me when Lisa and then Rick had to go off to Kindergarten. Lisa

---

[15] Interestingly, a 4th birthday party was going on in the same state for Kristen Cole and her twin sister Kathy. The girls were born in the same hospital on the same day as Robbie. Years later, Kristen would marry our son Rick.

took a long time to become convinced that going off to school meant a whole new world opening to her and that she would meet many new friends. She finally accepted this and the first day I left her at the school door and walked away, the tears were running down my face. And years later Rick begged me to take him back home each time I left him with his teacher. I tried unsuccessfully for months to convince him he too would enjoy school, and I cried every day when I walked away from him. He finally accepted the idea when he found a buddy in his class that didn't take to this school business very well either. They found comfort in each other and so soon they both forgot they didn't like it, especially when recess rolled around and they could play kickball outside. Suddenly, school was okay.

But when it was time to take Mike to school, I woke up with an extra spring in my step, and handing him off to the teacher who would be responsible for sitting on him until 2:30, I exited the building with a song in my heart and a goofy grin on my face. For at least a few hours I would have a reprieve. Talk about kids being different.

When Michael was about two years old, I had a day that was particular trying. Having three little ones under the age of seven is not often easy and my youngest was being perfectly horrible for the whole day. That night I bathed the kids and got them to bed early and was sitting in the kitchen smoking a cigarette to calm my nerves when Dick walked in the back door. I hadn't realized that night had fallen and Dick was surprised to see me sitting there in the dark. When he asked me what was wrong, I broke into tears and said just one word "Michael!" He knew. He understood. But luckily for me and all mothers of the world, kids grow up, change and level out. Mike did that and turned out to be the one to keep us all smiling with his antics as he grew. On more than one occasion, I thought my brother Vernon had come back into my life.

Chapter 22

Lights, Camera, Action All Over Again

***"The apple doesn't fall very
far from the tree"***

    Rick and Mike both needed to have a great sense of humor and a lot of patience as their sister Lisa tried her best to use them to suit her needs. Lisa would have been good on Stuart Street during the days of the Judy Garland - Mickey Rooney shows I was involved in. She too had a wild imagination and the target of this imagination was her two brothers.
    Dick and I did not have a lot of money as I chose not to work again fulltime until Michael was in school. Consequently we could not afford to go out often, and so movies and dinners were a very rare treat. But we had entertainment within our walls, compliments of Lisa's flare for theatrics. On numerous occasions, she would gather up her brothers and take them upstairs. Dick and I would hear much giggling and banging of closets and doors. We always knew that a "play" was in the process and the kids were finding the appropriate costumes. Finally, with a drum roll off her tongue, Lisa would enter the room and make a grand announcement that a show was about to begin. This was Dick's and my cue to take a seat and wait for the action to start.
    On one such occasion, Michael came in dressed as a cat with a long tail, purring on all fours followed by Rick adorned with one of my old wigs, a dress and my high heels. Lisa would ask them to perform or recite, and on cue they would respond to their director's orders. Another time they might be ghosts under my white sheets, or cast members of

the Wizard of Oz using Dick's old clothes. Our kids would be transformed into animals, babies, men, women (transvestites on many occasions) and anything else Lisa's mind could conjure up. I would take photos and for many years they held a special place in our photograph album. Then as Rick and Mike grew older and saw the spectacle their sister had made of them, many of the photos disappeared. I suspect they were frightened that they would end up in the hands of schoolmates or even worse, potential girlfriends.

Lisa, Rick and Mike got along pretty well and inner bickering was very rare and not tolerated on the few times it did rear its ugly head. Our kids were lucky in that Cooper Street was flooded with over fifty kids within our own block for many years. They only had to go out the back door or next door to find a playmate of their age. This was in the days where no one locked their doors and each family looked out for the neighbor's children.

When Rick and Mike would wander out the back door of our house at the age of 5 and 6, it was to go only a few doors down to the Guyton's house or next door to the Feisthamel's. I knew that they would happily play with their friends that lived there and would be watched by the parents who kept a close eye on their own kids as well as mine. And the same was true in reverse. When our kids played out back of our house and were visited by their friends, those kids came in for the same cookies and milk as ours did and used our bathrooms and had their noses wiped right along with ours. It was the way all children were raised in the 60's and 70's and it was comforting to know that all kids were everybody's kids.

When the Doe kids got a little older, the street games were played in earnest. These were Kick the Can and the other games I mentioned earlier but others were added as they grew. But now to explain the Hot Beans and Butter game.

While Lisa usually hung on the front porch talking with her friends until bedtime, her brothers would play the street games with the neighborhood kids. They loved to play out until it got a little dark, as this made the Hide and Seek games more interesting. So in the summertime, they were given a little leeway and could stay out until dusk.

One summer I noticed that often, when Rick and Mike would come in to get ready for their baths, I would notice bruises or small welts on their arms or legs. But they never acted as if anything bad had happened and in fact were very excited about the outcome of the evening's games. I asked Mike one night what game they had been playing that was causing so many bruises. He simply replied "Oh, it's called Hot Beans and Butter." Feeling it was time for a description of this game, he and Rick told me as I listened in horror that this was a game where, if you got caught, you were slugged with a branch or hose or anything that would hurt. I was outraged! There was no more Hot Beans and Butter nonsense after that night much to the disappointment of the boys. They found that to be a right manly little game. To this day, Mike tries to get a rise out of me by mentioning it.

When we left Cooper Street after living there for over forty years, it was with much trepidation and sadness but necessary for Dick's health. It was more than just moving from a home. We moved from memories that our kids to this day recall in laughter when they get together. Lisa, Rick and Mike played in Cooper Street homes, yards and roads. They climbed its trees, knew the back of all of the houses, had scampered through the shortcuts to and from school, played with the kids in almost every house and their wonderful memories were our wonderful memories too. To this day I hear so often from the now thirty-nine to forty-five year old former classmates of my kids, how the Doe's house was *the* house to go to.

Their parents knew they were looked after and all their friends would be there. I have to thank all our neighbors who most likely endured unimaginable problems caused by these same kids tipping over their garbage cans during Hide and Seek and listening to the noise and squeals of bicycle brakes in their driveways. They also must have turned up the volume of their television sets to drown out the cheerleading practicing of Lisa and her girlfriends who desperately wanted to qualify for the school's cheerleading squad. And the pickup basketball games in the driveway and football games in the road must have been loud and annoying to any neighbors wanting to sit down for a quiet evening in front of their TV sets.

And I'm so thankful that when our kids were younger and they and their friends ran up and down our house stairs or slid down its banisters or hung from a haphazardly erected monkey bar in the bedroom, that I wasn't into serious redecorating or worrying about how the house looked. I *know* how the house looked. It looked lived in. It looked loved in. Looking back, I wouldn't have had it any other way. However, don't try that in my house today!

Chapter 23

Eric Joseph Doe

Born and Died July 2, 1970

    I have recently read that there is only a 4-8% chance of a second occurrence of placenta previa. And in 1961 as a way of comforting me, my physician told me at the occasion of my first physical exam after the loss of Susan Kathleen, that it had a very small chance of ever happening to me again. So after having had that happen and having since given birth again to two healthy sons who were now six and four years of age, I had no reason to worry when I found myself expecting again for the fifth time.
    This baby was not due for another three months and was expected to arrive in October of 1970. I was not prepared for the hemorrhaging that woke me early in the hours of July 2nd. When I was admitted to the hospital, I was prepared for the intense labor once again but it was thankfully short-lived. In fact I was all alone when I realized I was about to give birth. There was no nurse or doctor around. I remember waking up in a room away from all the other expectant mothers. It was a hot and humid night and the window at the foot of the bed was open and a wind blowing over my sheets. I wasn't sure why I woke up at this particular moment but I suddenly knew that I was about to give birth. I remember yelling out "Dr. Baker!" at the top of my lungs. He had been sleeping in a nearby room and I heard him running towards my room and asking a nurse who was out of my sight, "Was that you that called me?" "No," was her reply, "It was Mrs. Doe."
    Dr. Baker was now in front of me, surveying the scene and he announced that he wouldn't be

taking me into the delivery room. And so there in that small side room, with a view of a full moon from the window at the foot of my bed, the baby was born. There was no cry, no sound except for the rustle of the nurse's uniform. Obviously the baby had been placed in a bassinette to the right of me and when the doctor asked me if I would like to see my son, I weakly answered "No." This was the second time I had ever been asked that question and both times I had said no. Occasionally to this day I second guess my decision. But if I had seen the little one-pound, one ounce girl or my new one pound, two ounce boy, their images would still be embedded in my mind and I don't know if I could deal with that.

    We named him Eric Joseph, a name that Dick and I had both chosen just a few short weeks earlier. As with Susan's death earlier and again with this death, Dick was the only one present at the small committal service that the undertaker held at Glenwood Cemetery. Dick didn't want anyone else to be there. He did say later that before the burial, he saw the undertaker carry a small figure covered by a diaper into another room and he knew that was our son being prepared for his burial. Dick was very sad when he told me that and he chose to never speak about the babies again.

    About a month or so after Eric's birth when I had Michael at our pediatrician's office for a visit, Dr. Sturtz talked about the baby I had just lost.

    "You know Kathy, the chances that he would have serious problems with an under-developed lung was very real if he had lived."

    He went on to say that brain abnormalities were also a real possibility.

    "Babies should not be born that early." is how he summed up our meeting.

    I have such learned that because of the quality and availability of neonatal intensive care units in most hospitals, babies born today at 24 weeks as was Susan and Eric, have a 40-50% chance of survival. But back in the 60's and 70's, the chance for survival at this age of gestation was almost nil. This is small consolation but what mother would want a child to live for days or months with severe neurological or lung disorders, lingering on a machine for each and every breath?

They were born, they were baptized and God is now taking care of them until we are reunited again some day.

Chapter 24

Parenting, Partying, Having Fun

Or - *How to survive on no money*

     Raising three kids in the 60's and 70's was much different than today. I was not a "Soccer Mom"; Dick and I did not follow our kids around on a daily basis to catch their every accomplishment. When the boys were very young, we'd take them to their ball games and watch from the sidelines and cheer them on. But as they grew and had tons of practices and many games at various fields, schools and cities, we did not feel pressured to attend each and every one of them, breathless over the wonderment that they could catch or throw a ball. In other words, we did not teach them that the sun rose and set on them. Today's parents probably would call this cruel but I prefer to think of it as letting your kids have a life! That's not to say that we ignored them. High school games were very exciting to watch and we tried to attend all that we possibly could. Both Rick and Mike played football and basketball for IHC[16] and both had an opportunity to play in the Syracuse's Carrier Dome when the IHC football team made it to the sectionals. This was a special treat for them and us. Lisa was a cheerleader for most of her high school years and it was even more exciting for me to watch her, realizing that I cheered for the same alma mater many years earlier.
     But when the kids were young and still in grade school, we did not have a lot of money and

---

[16] Immaculate Heart Academy (IHA) was changed to Immaculate Heart Central School (IHC) and moved to a new building in the 1970's.

170

therefore trips to Florida, the Carolina's and other sources of wonder were out of the question for us. So we decided we needed to get imaginative and make our own fun. Luckily, my sister Margaret and her husband Charlie and their brood were pretty much in the same boat as Dick and I. It was also fortunate that our kids were close in age to their kids – the first half of their kids, that is. The Sexton's had their first four kids, Laura, Linda, Robb and Ron early on. Theresa and Ann were much later so our kids did not have the chance to grow up with them but they do remember them as toddlers hanging around when both groups of older kids got together. So we decided to make our own fun and at the drop of a hat, the Doe's and Sexton's would spend nights, weekends and outings together. Rick and Mike loved playing with Robb and Ron, and Lisa got along famously with Laura and Linda. The adults played card games, smoked, drank a few beers and had tons of laughs. When I think of "the good old days," these memories quickly come to mind.

So because money was in short supply and exotic vacations not possible, Margaret and I decided to become creative and thus we devised a great plan for "alone time," something much needed by both couples. We created "Mini-Vacations" and went on them off and on for several years. It went something like this....Dick and I would bring the Sexton kids into our home for a weekend, allowing Charlie and Margaret the opportunity to do whatever they wanted; childless for a few days. Oh, the joy of that! They would go somewhere in the car for the day without four kids fighting in the back seat. They might stop for lunch (too expensive for eating dinner out) and then shop for a steak or special meal to bring home. Then the two of them would have that night and the whole next day before we'd drop their gang back to them. When it was Dick's and my turn, we'd settle on a weekend, drop our kids off to the

Sextons' and start the whole process all over again. The beauty of this arrangement was that not only did the grownups get something wonderful out of this, but so did the kids. Our kids loved going there and their kids loved coming to our house. Whenever I would share these details with friends, they would marvel at what a great arrangement it was and would often duplicate this mini-vacation with their own friends and family.

Chapter 25

Thomas L. Taylor
February 9, 1933 – February 3, 1990
The loss of another sibling

The death of our beloved brother Tom was hard on everyone. He was just the most lovable guy in the world. He so enjoyed music and making people laugh. He had a great singing voice and could yodel with the best of them.

As a small child, I would look up to him because he was only six years older than I was and would often include me in his games. As a teenager, I thought her was pretty cute and my girlfriends did too. He liked to wear his blonde hair in a big pompadour style which was pretty popular in the early 50's. He was also very much into clothes, not unlike his older brother Jack.

In one of the letters that Tom wrote to Olga which was chronicled in the book "*Letters to Olga*," Tom would go on and on regaling about a new shirt or other article of clothing that he had just acquired. And in another letter, he pleads to Olga and Bill....

> *January 28, 1952*
> *"Hey I wish you would do something for me... If you happen to see a beautiful, unusual shirt down there, I wish you would get it for me and bring it back when you come. I've looked all over town for a bright, yellow shirt with a different style like zippers instead of buttons.*
> *My size is 14 ½ - 15. Oh Hell, you can see all I've got to do around here is to look for unusual clothes to pass time away. By the way, I'll pay you when you get home."*

Obviously he was still waiting word on the shirt three months letter, as witnessed in this next letter to Olga...

> April 3, 1952
>
> "About that shirt – use your own judgment on a color and price. I know I'd like it, so long as it's unusual."

I have to laugh when I think about his penchant for zippered shirts in his youth because to the day he died, that was still his style of choice.

Tom chose to leave high school before graduating in favor of working at odd jobs in and around Watertown. Always the wanderlust, he decided to enlist in the Army and served in Korea during the conflict of the 1950's. He returned home for a while but eventually he moved to New Jersey, got married, later divorced and moved back to Watertown. Tom had tons of friends mainly because his outlook on life was contagious and almost everyone that knew him loved him and became his friend. He could have you in stitches while telling you stories of people he had come in contact with or relating a new joke he had just heard.

Like his older brother Jack before him, Tom enjoyed drinking too much. In later years, this disease necessitated several trips to the hospital and he was in and out several times before his last visit. I remember his being in the ICU of Mercy Hospital for a few days before he died. His room overlooked the helicopter pad which was used to transport critically ill patients before being admitted to the hospital. Tom was very ill and would wake for only a few minutes at a time and finally he remained in a coma. But one afternoon when he was resting and I sat near his bedside, a huge Army helicopter carrying an injured soldier from the local army base touched down. The racket outside of his window was fierce and Tom awoke and tried to sit up. He looked around the room frantically as if trying to find something. I remember wondering what was bothering him so much and tried to calm him down. I truly believe he was re-living some of his Korean War days and perhaps he might have been looking for his rifle. The fear in his eyes was palpable. I kept telling him over and over again what was going on and finally he believed me and went back to sleep.

On the day of the night that he died, I, along with some of my brothers and sisters, visited Tom in his hospital room. When I left at about seven that night I had a feeling that he would not last much longer. I made a promise to myself to go home, get some sleep and come back around one in the morning to see how he was doing. I told Dick of my plans and went to sleep, thinking the alarm clock would awaken me. I had not set the clock correctly and in the early morning hours, the phone rang and it was the hospital announcing that Tom had passed away. Olga, Vern, Alice and Bill were also called and we all met in his hospital room, a sad collection of siblings.

The task of informing Mom that her youngest son had passed away fell to Olga and me. We visited Mom in her apartment early the next morning as she was just putting coffee on her stove. She took one look at us and knew something was very wrong. I don't think I'll ever forget the look on her face when we informed her that her son had died.

Except for Mom, Tom's death affected no one greater than his brother Vern. They were close as youngsters and almost inseparable as adults working together, partying together, singing and laughing at the same jokes. Tom's death took away a little part of Vern. But thank God for our faith. How could we as humans, exist from one day to another without believing that we will all meet again in Heaven? I know there will be a great reunion when we Taylor's reunite with Mom, Dad and our brothers and the sister we never got to know.

Chapter 26

Mary Cecelia Ward Taylor
February 8, 1900 – June 6, 1995
An orphan no more

Mom lived to see her 95th birthday, with the last two years of her life spent in the Mercy Hospital Nursing Home. This was at first hard for her to get used to, but being able to get on the elevator and ride down two floors to the hospital chapel for noon Mass, made the loss of her freedom a bit easier.

She pretty much was the hit of the forth floor, namely because she had control of her mental faculties. So many of the residents were Alzheimer's patients, or if not, they suffered from other forms of dementia. But not Mom; she was still as sharp as a tack.

I remember being with her on one occasion shortly after she entered the nursing home. The hospital physician visited her room and began asking me certain things about Mom who was sitting next to him.

"I see by your mother's chart that she has been taking medicine for her thyroid condition since 1990."

He got no further than that, when Mom spoke up, corrected him on the year and then further filled him on the details of her operation for that problem and the ensuing problems she encountered. He looked at her smiled.

"Well, Mrs. Taylor I can see that you're someone to be reckoned with. I saw on your chart that you're in your nineties and assumed you might not remember all that much."

She went on to let him know in no uncertain terms that she was still here, had all her faculties and the doctor could talk directly to her, thank you very much!

About a month before she died, Mom had a Transient Ischemic attack (TIA). I received a call from the nursing home on-call physician who told me that she had a TIA and that they usually were precursors to a full blown stroke. He would put her on blood thinning medicines but we should not be surprised if she had a stroke within a short period of time. When I went up to visit her immediately after receiving that call, she explained that she had rung her call bell to summon the nurse because the side of her face and her hands felt numb. Luckily she did not suffer any additional symptoms and for a while seemed her old self.

On June 4th, I got a phone call from the same doctor who started out by saying "I'm sorry to have to tell you this Mrs. Doe, but your mother suffered a serious stroke. This will probably result in her death so you should let the rest of the family know." *(At this time, Olga and I were listed as the primary people to call if needed by the nursing home. This is why I received both of these calls. If Olga was not at home, they would call me or vise versa.).*

I contacted Olga and we immediately went to Mom's room and were terribly saddened to see the condition she was in. She always welcomed us when we entered her room and would be so happy to see family. But now she lay there in a comatose state and we were not prepared for that sight. The rest of the family was called and for the next two days, a bedside vigil was held. We prayed the rosary aloud, held her hand and talked to her. She knew we were there even though she could not communicate. One time, I took her hand and made the sign on the cross on her forehead and chest. Because I was on the side of her, I mistakenly made the sign of the cross in reverse. Slowly, with no other outward sign that she was aware, she moved her hand to her face and made the sign of the cross the right way. Even close to death, she was alert enough to pray correctly.

Olga, Margaret and I were with Mom on the night she died. I was trying to sleep on a bed outside her door in the hallway and Olga and Margaret were in chairs next to Mom. We had all been sitting with her for hours and hours throughout the past few days and were exhausted. Olga suddenly awoke and looked at Mom and woke Margaret first to tell her that she did not see Mom breathing. Then Olga came out into the hall to awaken me. We at first were rather sad that Mom died with none of us awake holding her hand but realized that this was God's plan for Mom and so who were we to be concerned at how He chose to take her home?

It was about 12:15 a.m. on June 6th when we called the nurse and Mom was pronounced dead; therefore her death certificate states June 6th as the date she expired. Both Olga and Margaret felt that she most likely had been dead since before midnight and the actual date of her death was probably the 5th of June. I don't concur with them and because of the following incidents; I have my own reasons for believing she did indeed die on the 6th.

A few days after Mom's death, I was at Sacred Heart church rectory to buy a Mass card. One of the Missionary of the Sacred Heart's brothers, Brother Michael, asked me on what date my mother died.

"June 6th, I told him.

"Oh, the feast of St. Norbert, a wonderful saint," he replied.

I asked him how he knew that without referring to a Catholic calendar and he told me that one of his specialties was to know much about the saints, their dates of deaths and their accomplishments when they were living.

I was very curious and wanted to know more about St. Norbert. Brother Michael had a lot of information about him and I liked what I was hearing. When I came home I looked on the computer for more information about this saint and found something that convinced me that Mom did indeed die on this great man's feast day. In addition to the many inspiring stories attributed to St. Norbert, he was also known for helping the priests prepare to celebrate Mass. He helped with their garments and prepared in any way he could to assist the celebrants. Immediately my mind went back to the years and years that Mom had done just that. When living across the street from St. Patrick's church for example, it was Mom who daily walked across the street and helped the altar boys get dressed. She buttoned their cassocks, combed their hair and then after Mass, it was Mom who brought home the priest's vestments and altar linens to be washed and starched and returned to the church for the next day's Mass. It helped convince me that she died on St. Norbert's feast day. It just seemed to fit.

Another reason I was sure of this was because everything spiritual I have ever read about the death of a person leads me to the belief that a soul does not *immediately* leave the body. This is why so many people have been resuscitated long after death has been pronounced in many cases. Death is not immediate and according to many books on the subject, we have an opportunity to see our souls as God does.

According to the book "*The Amazing Secret of the Souls in Purgatory,*" by Sr. Emmanuel of Medjugorje, it is stated that immediately after death, we are visited by Our Blessed Mother and the saints. This extremely interesting book was written by Sr. Emmanuel after many interviews with Maria Simma, an elderly and deeply religious woman of Sonntag, Austria. Maria Simma has been visited by the souls in Purgatory for many years, after a lifelong dedication to praying for their release from Purgatory. She states that we do indeed have one last chance to make right any sins of our life. In answer to this specific question posed by Sister Emmanuel:

"Maria, at the moment of death, is there a time in which the soul still has the chance to turn towards God before entering eternity – a time, if you like, before apparent death and real death?"

Maria's answer was definite.

"Yes, yes, the Lord gives several minutes to each one, in order to regret his sins and to decide: I accept or I do not accept to go see God. We see a film of our lives.

So because of this, I believe we go through a litany of our life. We see all the good we did to one another and have a time also to reflect on all the times we turned away from God. I think that this takes time, time for a person to see that film in our mind that Maria speaks about. So death of the soul is most likely not instantaneous and in fact may take much longer than we would assume.

In addition, I have another reason to believe that it was indeed meant for Mom to be alone when she passed away.

For years and years, Mom read her *Pieta* prayer book faithfully[17]. Many of the prayers she recited daily. One of them was the prayer dedicated to consecrating the last two hours of one's life to the Most Holy Virgin. She prayed this prayer religiously. After her death, I looked in my own *Pieta* book and read the words of that prayer; convinced more than ever that it was God's will that my sisters and I slept as Mom lay dying. In essence, that prayer reads....

> *O Mary, I beg thee to accept the petition my heart is going to make. It is for my last moments...*
> *Dear Mother, I wish to request thy*

---

[17] Published by Miraculous Lady of the Roses, Hickory Corners, Michigan

protection and maternal love so that in the decisive instant, thou wilt do all thy love can suggest on my behalf.

To thee O Mother of my soul, I consecrate the last two hours of my life. Come to my side as I receive my last breath and when Jesus has cut the thread of my days, tell Jesus, presenting to Him my soul... "I LOVE IT." That word alone will be enough to procure for me, the benediction of my God and the happiness of seeing thee for all eternity."

During the last two hours of Mom's life, we daughters slept close by while she was visited by Our Blessed Mother, who presented Mary Taylor's soul to Jesus, telling Him, "*I LOVE IT.*" I have no doubt of this.

Chapter 27

Harvey E. Taylor
September 14, 1923 – November 21, 2004
And yet another brother...

  Our oldest brother Harvey, known as "Red" to so many of his friends and some family members as well, was very ill for many years before he died in 2004. About six or seven years ago, he was told that his heart was so bad that he had only about two years to live. But he kept going and eventually even cancer claimed him as a victim. In the last few years of his life he was fed through a tube in his stomach but still made his rounds to visit friends and most specifically, veterans who were patients in the local hospitals.
  It was difficult to find someone as loyal to his country, and to those who fought to preserve it, as our brother Harvey. It was a rare Veteran's Day parade that didn't feature him marching with the local American Legion contingent. He did this until he became too ill to do so but his pride as a Legionnaire never wavered. Many ill veterans were visited by Harvey in the local hospitals and the V.A. hospitals in the area. You could definitely say that he took his patriotism seriously.
  Harvey entered the U.S. Army in 1943 and served with the Horse Cavalry. He lasted there for only five months until he was thrown by a horse and was medically discharged in September of the same year. For someone with such a short term in the military, or perhaps because of it, he remained a soldier all the rest of his life.

Chapter 28

The Long Wait

"I'm sorry but you need to contact Hospice"

We all know we're going to die... someday... when we're older and ready. It will be time; we'll be tired of living so long. We'll be feeble and will say that we've done all there is to do. We no longer will have anything to accomplish so it won't be so hard to accept.

Those are the plans of man; not God. Who knows who will have to suffer or if they will at all? Some people will slip quietly away, while others will endure much for a long time.

Dick never planned on that happening to him nor did I. But his lifelong passion for smoking cigarettes took away his capacity to breathe normally and stripped him of the simple pleasures of life and shortened it considerably.

When he was in his late 40's, Dick knew he had to give up smoking and he did. I had stopped smoking myself years earlier at age thirty before undergoing a hysterectomy. This was on my physician's suggestion and thankfully I never took up this nasty habit again. Dick found that stopping wasn't as hard as he had imagined and we were both glad that it was relatively easy for him.

The doctors had hinted on many occasions that he had the beginning of emphysema, a deadly disease that robs the lungs of obtaining all the oxygen needed to take a deep breath when needed. Emphysema patients are always breathing as if through a straw. And so when necessary, for example, to get up quickly from a chair or to run to the car in a rainstorm, it is always done so with that imagined straw in your mouth. A task that is hard to realize unless you've suffered it yourself.

As time went on and his breathing became more difficult, it became increasingly harder and harder for him to complete the tasks that he used to do so easily. Often I would watch him from the corner of my eye as he attempted to struggle to carry a heavy object and so I would "just happen" to have to go near him and would help him as if it were an afterthought. And when he would try to attempt the stairs in our cellar or the ones leading to our second floor bedroom, he would stop half way up and pretend to be examining something on the wall when all the time he was just taking time to get his second wind.

Things got so hard for him that we made an appointment with Dr. David Rechlin, a local and highly respected pulmonary physician. Dr. Rechlin scheduled a round of X-rays and breathing tests and when the results were all in, he advised us that Dick's lungs had deteriorated greatly. And so Dick began taking many new prescription medicines in an attempt to improve his lung function. The doctor also gave him an exercise prescription that allowed him to enroll in a cardio-rehab fitness class at the local hospital that was specifically created for those with lung and heart problems. The doctor explained to us that although nothing can halt the progression of emphysema; maintaining your health through diet and exercise can slow it down. And so off Dick went twice a week to the class for his exercise therapy. Unfortunately he would often be stricken with a bad cold or some sort of bug which would interrupt his progress and he would have to start at the beginning again.

Eventually he could no longer attend these classes. He just felt too winded to keep up and he promised the doctor that he would continue trying to stay fit by walking around the streets of our new home at Northland Estates.

We made the move from our large house to a smaller one, a six room doublewide home, primarily for Dick. It allowed him to no longer have to use stairs to go to the bathroom or to our bedroom. Now everything was on one floor and life became much easier for him. So he began attempting to walk around the streets of the park religiously until one day he went on his walk and did not return home as quickly as normal. I began to worry and looked out the windows of the front of our house as well as the rear. I could not see him so I went for a walk myself, with the intention of looking for him. I found him sitting on a large rock that bordered someone's property. His breathing was very labored and I asked him if he wanted me to go home and get the car but of course he would not allow that. He and I walked back slowly as we pretended to anyone sitting on their porch watching, that it was a lovely day to just stroll at a crawl pace. That was the last time he did any exercise of any kind.

Dick continued to go to the golf course, but more often than not, he'd have to give up on about the 13th or 14th hole. His good buddies, especially Budgo and Lou, would call me the same evening that Dick did not do so well and ask me how he was feeling. They would tell me how much he labored that day but that he would not give up until he just could not go any further.

In June of 2001, Dick developed a severe respiratory infection. He ended up on antibiotics and steroids in an attempt to open up his weakened lungs. He was very ill for over a week. We had to go back to the doctor for another physical and were hoping he had a magic bullet but weren't expecting too much. By the time his appointment rolled around, Dick was much worse. He could not stop coughing and just could not seem to kick this latest bug.

On June 27, 2001, Dr. Rechlin performed an extensive workup on Dick and his blood tests showed that his oxygen level was about 85 instead of his usual 95 or 96. The doctor spoke to Dick about signing up to have oxygen in our house which would provide relief whenever he needed it.

Before all this occurred, I would always accompany Dick on his trips to the doctor. There was always someone sitting in the waiting room wearing an oxygen mask while the ever present O^2 canister sat by their feet. On more than one occasion, Dick would say to me,

"You know Gaff, if I ever have to get to the point of wearing oxygen, I'll know it's all over. I pray to God that I never have to have it."

On July 28, 2001 a local home care company delivered the oxygen concentrator to our house. Plus a backup tank...and wheels for the backup tank...and canulas...and extra hoses...and pages of instructions on how to care for this equipment. I stood there looking at all of this wondering where I would put it all. Dick looked at it wondering how the rest of his life would be lived.

Three years earlier, in 1998, I had begun to keep a journal after hearing that it's a good idea for a person to record, at least occasionally, some of the events of their life. Little did I know then that it would become a way to document the changes in my husband's life, our life together and that of our children and grandchildren. The entry for the day the oxygen entered our life follows.

"Today, Marra's Home care delivered oxygen for Dick. It is a sad day as he always said he would hate to have to be dependant on oxygen for life. But his breathing has been terrible. Budgo told

me that Dick had been having very bad days on the golf course. Maybe the oxygen can help him on the course.

The plan is for Dick to use it only at night so that he can possibly wake up with more energy. I have a real fear of the unknown. Stupid as it sounds, I wonder if we can still travel? Can we go to Boston to see Rick and his family, carrying this oxygen concentrator around? Can we ever go back to Florida or South Carolina so he can golf with his buddies? Can we take oxygen on an airplane?

What about his golf? Will he be able to do that while wearing an oxygen tank? He would absolutely die if he could not longer golf. If I have fears, I can only imagine what goes through his mind."

    The following day I told Lisa and Mike that their father would now have oxygen to help him breath. As expected, they were very saddened by the news but felt that this could possibly give him new energy and could help his breathing a great deal.
    Rick was living in the Boston area at the time and so that morning I sat down at my computer to email him like I often did. I told him about the new development and how his father was accepting everything. When I email him, I can usually expect an answer the same day. But several days went by and I did not hear back. I assumed he was very busy but felt a little miffed that he did not respond to this latest development in his father's life.
    Finally, the next morning I received an email. This is what he had to say.

Mom –

    I received your message the day before yesterday about Dad needing to have oxygen in the house from now on and it upset me so much that I needed to take some time to respond.

    You know when I was a little kid, Dad was 10 feet tall to me. I always was impressed at how big his arms were and how much he could lift- (remember how he used to lay on the floor and have Mike and I lay on each arm?). Of course when you are only 5 and your Dad is 3 feet taller than you; you think he **is** 10 feet tall. But when we needed help with our paper route if it was pouring outside, Dad would pick up all the wet papers, throw them into the back of the car and drive us around. When either Mike or I got hurt, he would scoop us up in his arms and take us to you to fix our "boo-boo's" and you both would tell us it would be alright. The same when we fell asleep over at Grandma's house and he would come to bring us home. He would pick both of us up and lay us in the car.

    As I grew older and taller than Dad, it seemed to me that he had shrunk. In physical appearance he was no longer 10 feet tall, but he was still someone I looked up to even if I was actually taller than him.

    The real reason Dad was always ten feet tall to me was not what he looked like but who he was. He was always such a very devoted man to his children, to his wife and to God. Dad was a person that you could always count on, someone that had the highest morals and expected only the best from his kids. Through each event you two encountered, you both became larger and larger to us all.

  When Dad was laid off he didn't go around complaining about it but took other work to make up for it, and never once did we lack for anything during that time. As other events occurred, Dad had a choice to either roll over and play dead or to let it roll off his back and go on with life. And when he encountered Cancer he decided that he wasn't going to be house bound because he had to wear an appliance around his waist. Instead he took it as a challenge and even went to the hospital to cheer up another friend of his who was going through the same thing, even though Dad hated to do any type of public speaking.

  Though I do not look through the eyes of a 5 year old anymore and see my Dad as ten feet tall literally, he is still larger than life to me; someone I truly look up to and someone I am very proud to call my father no matter what. As he and you have done with everything else that has come your way, I am sure that you have already found the silver lining in this. In fact you even said it in the e-mail, "He is happy to be breathing easier again." And may I add, it's better than not being here at all. I pray every day that God will keep the both of you around for many, many years to come because I want my kids and grandkids to have the opportunity to know, love and admire the two of you as we do.

  Give Dad my love and I expect to hear a ton of funny stories about how three year old Makayla pulls on Dad's oxygen tube all the time or how you stand on it and cut off his

oxygen when you get mad at him, or how Mike has figured out a way to hook it up to a beer can.
    Dad has always been an inspiration to me and I hope he is for a very long time to come. I love and miss you both.

    Love,
    Rick

    With his new and very important friend the O^2 tank, Dick continued to golf as many days as possible. Only the year before, he would golf about four days a week but now it became about two and then eventually it was one.
    Dick loved golf with a passion...it was more than a passion...it became his life. When he finally retired from his job as a tree trimmer with the local utility company, he was able to devote almost all his waking hours to this love of his. And I didn't mind because he would leave so early in the morning anyway and was usually back early in the afternoon, which was plenty enough time for us to do something together. Plus I figured if anyone could get that much joy out of something as silly as chasing a ball around 18 holes, why should I stop it?
    In addition to the love of playing the game, the wonderful friendships he had with his great buddies was something everyone should experience. Dick's golfing buddies were the cream of the crop. They looked after him, worried about him, cheered him on when he had a good game and came out to the house to visit him when he could no longer play the game. I got to love these guys as much as Dick did and still do.
    Interestingly, his introduction to this game was not until he was much older. As I stated earlier, he played all sports with ease. As a

youngster, he picked up a football for the first time and threw it across the backyard effortlessly. When pitched his first baseball, he'd hit it a country mile. But surprisingly he didn't pick up a golf club until he was in his 40's. A couple of his friends asked him to go golfing with them and he told them he didn't know how to golf but would like to give it a try. And so he and the friends went. Upon returning home Dick told me that he thought this game was a lot of fun and one he'd like to pursue when he could afford his own clubs and get a membership into one of the local golf clubs.

Only later did I learn from one of his buddies, that when they figured up their scores that day, he was shocked to learn that Dick had shot an 81 on his first attempt ever at the game.

And so Dick and the game of golf had an affair; one that would last until 2003 when he was forced to give it up. In that year, he began taking his portable oxygen tank with him wherever he went. The country club he belonged to was cordial enough to allow him to drive his golf cart closer to the greens than allowed by the course rules. So he became a familiar sight, a little man, stooped over so that he could draw more oxygen into his lungs, thinning grey hair blowing in the wind, sporting a portable oxygen tank over his back as he swung the ball a country mile.

One of my favorite stories ever about Dick has to do with his golfing with that damnable tank.

Just before he was forced to give up golfing, Dick was enjoying a game one day with his buddies. His foursome was on the putting green and all were waiting for one of the players to finish putting. Suddenly a ball came barreling at them and at the last minute they heard "Fore." They were all pretty livid because it was plain to see that the guy who had just driven his ball had no right to do so. But Dick was the maddest of all. One of his beloved friends almost got clobbered as the ball came swishing past his head.

Later when the errant golfer came closer, he tried to apologize but my husband would have none of it. Dick started yelling at the guy, telling him he was a "jerk and could have killed someone." As the story goes, a few hours later this errant golfer was overheard in the clubhouse telling some of his buddies that he almost hit a golfer. He went on to say that he tried to apologize but, "This little guy with gray hair and an oxygen tank strapped to his back almost chewed my ass off." Yup, don't mess with Dickie Doe or his friends.

Our visits with Dick's pulmonary physician became more frequent. Anytime he started to cough or sneeze, it necessitated that he quickly start a round of antibiotics. For Dick to get a severe infection, especially respiratory, could mean death because of his weakened lungs.

At one of our regular meetings with the lung doctor that we both were so fond of, he approached the subject of lung volume reduction surgery (LVR). The doctor explained that LVR surgery might be a possibility for Dick and he would investigate it for us. Lung volume reduction surgery is an innovative emphysema treatment that removes 20 to 30 percent of the lung tissue most damaged by emphysema. This allows the remaining, less diseased portion of the lung more room to function resulting in easier breathing. This is not a cure but, in selected patients, the procedure provides an alternative to a lung transplant. It also is appropriate for patients who are not eligible for lung transplantation. The goal is to set the clock back five years. Patients must have severe emphysema and meet strict requirements to be considered a candidate for the surgery.

And so Dick began a round of intensive tests, plus paperwork and office visits to determine if he was eligible. Dr. Rechlin finally summed up the results in this manner.

"Well Dick, you meet some of the criteria but not all. You are definitely sick enough to have the treatment but I'm not sure if you are well enough to go through it. I want to do some more testing to make sure you could survive this."

We also began to find out that this surgery, still considered experimental, was not covered by insurance. The cost was at least $65,000 and so those who were considered a good candidate for it had to be enrolled in a lung reduction trial program. It was a program that necessitated that the patient attend many studies out of town and possibly for a long period of time. We decided to wait to see if they would take him in this program, although deep down, neither of us felt that he had a good chance due to his rapid decline in lung function. We kept saying that this was definitely a "damned if you do and damned if you don't situation."

It was about this time and with much sadness that Dick and I had "*the talk.*" It was one I dreaded but knew had to take place. When I would see him drive back into our driveway after golfing, trying to get his clubs out of the trunk and carry them up the steps, huffing and puffing every step of the way, I knew it was time. I would always ask him how he golfed and the reply lately had been that he only finished four or five holes before he had to quit. It got to the point that he suffered for the next couple of days after his attempts to golf. I knew it was taking a toll on him but also knew he was desperate not to have to give up.

Finally the time came, and at breakfast one morning and over our coffee, I asked him if he felt it was time to devote his strength and energy to breathing as opposed to going out on days that were sometimes humid, sometimes cold and rainy and always so hard on him. He got angry and defensive, stood up and took his coffee out to his shed where I'm sure he mulled over what I had just stated. That night I felt that he was quieter than usual and I wasn't sure what decision, if any, he was making in his mind.

The next morning he looked at me and said, "You know Gaff, you're right. As much as I hate to admit it, this game is killing me. But Geez, it's hard to give up."

At that, he put his head in his hands and started to cry. I went over to where he was sitting on the counter bar stool and sat next to him and took his hand. Then I told him there were other things he could still do. He had always kept the statistics for the league and he could continue doing that on the computer. Plus he could go out to the course every Tuesday and be with the guys when they ended their game. He seemed to accept that and told me that he wanted to have the guys out to the house for a meeting. He would let them know in person and asked me to host a little party for them. Crying now too, I told him I would call Lou and have him round up the guys and invite them out for drinks and snacks.

Several days later, his good buddies came, giving Dick and me hugs and settling in our new sunroom for the "meeting." We tried to make the occasion festive; some cold beers, Croghan bologna, cheese curd and lots of golf stories; the staple of any get-together with these guys. In a little while, Dick said he had something he wanted to tell them and so he informed them he would have to give up the game for health reasons. But typical of Dick, fearing this would make them feel badly, he went on to describe ways in which he could still stay involved.

But you could see that the guys were sad to hear this news. They loved Dick so much and felt the league wouldn't be the same without him. And later on, at season's end, to prove how much they thought of him, they renamed the league the "*Dick Doe Over The Hill Golf League.*"

And so began a new life for Dick. It started out not being too much worse. He had his good days and not so good days.

In July of 2003, he had a horrible breathing spell and ended up going to the ER by ambulance. He was in the ICU for five days and on a respirator. When he was finally good enough to come home, he was never as strong as before he went in. He spent most of his time putting puzzles together or playing on his computer. He'd call his golf buddies and ask them how the league was doing and when he'd hang up, he would be so sad but never complained.

In December of that year, he contracted pneumonia and back to the hospital by ambulance he went again. He and our whole family spent Christmas in his private room in the hospital. He opened a card from all of us stating that he would have a brand new computer in his bedroom waiting for him when he came home. Dick loved to tinker with card games on the computer plus he would be able to work on the handicap program for the golf league. He was pretty excited.

The pneumonia Dick was fighting turned out to be a staph infection and was very difficult to clear up. His physicians wanted him to stay hospitalized until it was completely gone but Dick became desperate to come home. He had been in for over 27 days! After much pleading with his doctors, they told us that if I could learn how to administer his IV antibiotic treatment at home they would release him. I was terrified of having to be responsible for this but knew Dick would be

196

hospitalized weeks longer if I didn't learn, so I agreed to take on the task.

So on December 30th, we came home bundled down with so many medicines and instructions that I was truly overwhelmed. But if I thought that was frightening, I soon learned that it would get much worse.

In the afternoon, the doorbell started ringing and in came oxygen equipment, a bi-papp machine to help him sleep and then the IV pole, dozens of packages of needles and medications that I would inject; albeit terrifyingly so. Soon the Public Health Nurse came to witness whether or not I had learned the technique of opening the vials of antibiotic, shaking them as I did to get rid of any air bubbles that could be dangerous, check Dick's IV site in his hand to be sure it wasn't infected, and all the other little tricks they had taught me. I was happy when she left until I woke to my alarm at 2:00 a.m. to administer his first dose.

Poor Dick. He was so patient and had so much faith in my knowing what I was doing. My hands shook the first few times but eventually the desire I had to become a nurse as a youngster kicked in and I became the Florence Nightingale I never officially got to be.

Four days later with a new respiratory problem, he was back in an ambulance on the way to the hospital. Happy New Year Dick!

Once again, they adjusted his medicines and IV's (thank God it was in their hands again) and once again they got him stabilized. Ten days later they said he could go home which surprised me as he seemed so sick. But his doctor told me it was not because Dick was better that he was being discharged, but because there was nothing else they could do for him there. Dick's three primary physicians had met, poured over his charts, his history and this rapid decline in his health and then asked for me to contact my children and meet with a case worker in one of the hospital conference rooms. It was there that we were informed they would sign Dick up for Hospice care. Lisa, Rick and Mike asked all the questions I was too afraid to ask. It was just such a surreal moment and so very frightening.

Thus began Dick's and my new life; one consisting of licensed practical nurses to bathe and dress him daily, weekly registered nurses to access his health, and monthly social workers to see how we were both doing emotionally.

Sadly, the grandchildren began to see Poppy as someone who was always lying prone in bed and never getting out of his pajamas or playing with them any more. Mike's daughter Makayla once asked him, "Poppy, when are you going to get better so you can get out of that bed?" A question we all wish had a promising answer.

For the grandchildren, there is much about their grandfather they will never know. The older ones in time may forget how their Poppy used to carry them around and swing them over his head.

They may not remember the muscles that bulged from his arms, toned in his early years when he had his sons swing from them. They'll never know about the wrestling matches he had with those same sons. Matches that caused his sons to beg for help, even when he was taking on two teenage boys at a time. And none of them saw the strength their grandfather portrayed when he braved the front on a freezing night in Korea, feeding heavy mortar into huge guns, defending his and his platoon's position; an act that won him a Bronze Star.

Will they forget the "special-ness" of this grandfather; the one who carried their grandmother over the threshold on their wedding night, vowing to take care of her forever and ever?

Right now, they see only a man in his pajamas, and they help him plug in his breathing machine or try to learn to take his blood pressure. They assist him when the bell goes off if he needs something. But they love him no less than if they witnessed the tough and rugged Dick Doe. For he is their Poppy, a beloved figure who embraces them a little harder now and never forgets to tell them that he loves them when they leave. I pray they never forget him.

As I write this last chapter of my memoirs, it has been over a year since we were told he had six months to live. But that makes more sense than anything to me. Of course he would outlive their estimates. They do not know who they are dealing with here. This is a man who was a superb athlete from childhood; one who met challenges head on his whole life. One who defied his senior officer in Korea telling him he would not need to write a goodbye letter; he would not die that night. And so his fight goes on. Sometimes he is sad when he realizes the things he cannot do. When he hears of one of his grandchildren playing a sport, he dies inside because he cannot be on the sideline to watch and root him or her on as his father once did for his children. And when the family has get-togethers and much frivolity abounds, he hates it when he has to ask me to take him back to his room for his much needed breathing treatment. But complain...never! It is not in his makeup to complain. As he once told me when I asked him why he always told his buddies that he is "fine, just fine, thank you" when in fact he had a terrible day, his response was simple; "Who wants to hear about people's illnesses? Everyone has a problem and no one wants to hear about mine." That sums him up very simply. It's what has kept him going for months and months longer than three physicians had expected. It's what I suspect will keep him going for a lot longer. And for that, his family and friends are very happy.

Chapter 29

A Letter to My Children

Dear Lisa, Rick and Mike:

As I stated in the beginning of this book, the reason I took it on as a project was that it would most likely give me something to do as I become increasingly housebound with your father. But as I started recalling my memories, I realized that reaching back into a childhood full of so many emotions may be painful at times, but for the most part, their remembrance was very comforting.

I wanted to share some of those emotions with you, thus the book. I certainly am no great author but I believe you don't have to be a skilled writer to be a storyteller. We all do that on a regular basis. We relate funny, sad and poignant things all the time to others. But to sit down at a computer and try to put thoughts into some sort of order and at the same time to be of interest to others was for me a real challenge. However, as the story grew, I found myself eager to get back at it because conjuring up these memories helped me to relive some really great times in my life.

I had and still have a great family. The Taylor clan was one reared in strong beliefs of God, patriotism and self reliance. There was no coddling and babying and we were all expected to do what needed doing. It was assumed that we would obey authority and we always knew we were responsible for our own actions...a mantra that I have preached to you kids all your lives.

I have not written much about your days of growing up; just touched on a few incidents that fit in well at certain times. I want you to have your own memories, flavored by your own experiences. I hope that someday you will leave something similar to your children. After all, we all have lessons we have learned in our life that we have obtained by trial and error. We all become stronger for getting through the rough times and can draw on the good times to keep our remembrances joyful.

Conjuring up the memories of my childhood was like a movie reel being played in my brain. As soon as I would think of a situation and try to put it on paper, then another incident that reminded me of something similar would pop into my mind. It truly was entertaining to me to attend the movie in my head.

I had not expected to write an entire chapter on your father's illness; and in fact thought long and hard about whether or not I should include it. After all, this was intended to be about my growing up a Taylor and marrying and having you kids.

But even though you will always prefer to remember the healthier and more active Dick Doe, I felt that it was important for you to remember and teach your children about the man that went through so much in his later life but never lost his love for life and his family.

I hope you enjoyed reading about the story of my childhood and reaching adulthood and marrying the man who was responsible for all the good parts in you...your father.

Love Always,

Mom

Our Great Kids -1967
Rick, age 3, Lisa, age 7
and Mike age 2

Epilogue – June 2005

"Just because you know someone is going to die soon does not make their passing any easier." I had heard this said many times from various sources. People who had actually experienced this said these words to me and I had so many well meaning friends who warned me of this fact. Somehow I felt I was above this. After all, I had known for fifteen months that Dick was terminal and would not live much longer. I knew it; I believed it and still it shocked me when it became a reality.

The winter of 2005 was long, cold and very hard on Dick. He experienced so many setbacks, namely urinary tract infections which set him into such a state of decline that I braced myself for his eminent death. I don't know why I was so foolish as to not realize that he was so strong and stubborn and had such a desire to fight death until the last minute.

But eventually he became too weak to fight off these infections any longer. The wonderful people of Hospice began to warn me that these infections were taking a terrible toll on Dick's health and in late January and early February of 2005, their experienced proclamations became true. He began to slip into what I called a semi-coma. He would have days where he would be alert for several hours and he became what I referred to as "Silly Dick." He was so happy and easy-going at these times. He would infuriate me on these days because he was like a child trying desperately to tease and torment his parent.

For example, if I asked him what he wanted for lunch, he would tell me one thing and as I walked away to get it, he would ring his bell and inform me that he was just fooling and that he really wanted something entirely different. Then he would laugh and raise his arms straight up in the air and wiggle his fingers, beckoning me to come towards him. I would go to him and attempt to lay my head on his chest, harder to do now since the side rails of his bed needed to be permanently raised. He would just hold me and laugh and tell me he was just fooling and would give me a big hug and smile and tell me he loved me.

These were warm and tender moments with him but they soon diminished as he slept more and more. It took a lot of shaking and calling his name to get a response. I now took this as a sign that soon he would be sleeping all the time and it did happen just that way.

On the evening of February 17th, I told my children that it was obvious their father would not be here much longer. Stepping out for just a few minutes the next morning, they were not back in time when Dick passed away. I expressed my sorrow to them that they could not be there when their father took his last breath but they convinced me that this was the way it was meant to be – just him and me alone together. And so it was. With my hand in his and his eyes open for the first time in over a week, Dick took his last breath and slipped slowly and calmly into the hands of God.

This story of the Taylor family should not end on a sad note. Dick's contribution to the life of the youngest member of this family needed to be highlighted. Who we are born to, and the family we are raised in, contributes in a huge way to who we become as adults. But who we marry and share our lives with contributes to the next generation's views on life. Dick's life was dedicated to God, his family, his friends, his great love of sports and the desire to live each moment to its fullest. That is what he'd want his legacy to be.

When I decided to create a program that would be used at his funeral, I went on the Internet in search of the perfect poem that would sum up his life. After hours of fruitless searching, I found a poem entitled "*Afterglow*" and felt it was exactly what I was looking for. And so I placed it on the front cover, underneath his photo. I think it sums up perfectly, his joy for life.......

Richard L. Doe
July 31, 1932 – February 18, 2005

Afterglow

I'd like the memory of me to be a happy one.
I'd like to leave an afterglow of smiles
when life is done.

I'd like to leave an echo whispering
softly down the ways,
Of happy times and laughing times
and bright and sunny days.

I'd like the tears of those who grieve,
to dry before the sun
Of happy memories I leave when my life is done.

John A. Baker, Author

About The Author

Katherine (Kathy) Taylor Doe was born in West Carthage New York, the youngest of nine children, and has lived all of her life in Watertown, New York.

She holds two part time jobs – one as an adjunct computer instructor, teaching classes in the Continuing Education Department of the local community college, and as an office aide to a New York State Assemblyman.

This book was initially begun as a family history for her children and grandchildren and ended up being a tribute to her late husband, Richard L. Doe.

You may contact Kathy at kldoe@twcny.rr.com

ISBN 1425102891

Made in the USA
Middletown, DE
22 December 2015